UNLOCKING THE PROPHETIC MYSTERIES OF ISRAEL

UNLOCKING THE PROPHETIC MYSTERIES OF ISRAEL

JONATHAN BERNIS

Most Charisma House Book Group products are available at special quantity discounts for bulk purchase for sales promotions, premiums, fund-raising, and educational needs. For details, write Charisma House Book Group, 600 Rinehart Road, Lake Mary, Florida 32746, or telephone (407) 333-0600.

Unlocking the Prophetic Mysteries of Israel by Jonathan Bernis
Published by Charisma House
Charisma Media/Charisma House Book Group
600 Rinehart Road
Lake Mary, Florida 32746
www.charismahouse.com

Cover design by Justin Evans

Visit the author's website at www.jewishvoice.org.

Library of Congress Cataloging-in-Publication Data:
An application to register this book for cataloging has been submitted to the Library of Congress.
International Standard Book Number: 978-1-62999-140-5
E-book ISBN: 978-1-62999-141-2

First edition

17 18 19 20 21—987654321
Printed in the United States of America

This book is dedicated to my fellow leaders in Messianic Jewish ministry. Many of you have dedicated your lives to this work with very little recognition or support. You have endured the rejection of your parents, families, and friends to "follow the Lamb wherever He goes" (Rev. 14:4). God sees your labors, and they are not in vain. Never forget, in the end "all Israel will be saved" (Rom. 11:26). Keep pressing on, my dear comrades!

In memory of my beloved brother
Dave Bernis
April 15, 1958–January 21, 2017

CONTENTS

Acknowledgments xi

Introduction xiii

Chapter 1 **Key One:** The Seed Promise 1

Chapter 2 **Key Two:** The Abrahamic Blessing 25

Chapter 3 **Key Three:** The New Covenant 45

Chapter 4 **Key Four:** The Restoration of Jerusalem 65

Chapter 5 **Key Five:** The Gospel to the Jew First 95

Chapter 6 **Key Six:** Bringing Life From the Dead 117

Chapter 7 **Key Seven:** The Restoration of All Things 135

Conclusion:
Fight the Good Fight 163

Notes 171

ACKNOWLEDGMENTS

I WISH TO THANK my dedicated staff at Jewish Voice, especially my executive leadership team. Ezra, Troy, Ellen, Joseph, Michael and Matt, growing and learning with you this past year has been an honor and a joy.

Thanks to Angela Smith, Carly Berna, and Charlene McClellan for all your support with the myriad of details, and to Dave Wimbish for your great writing and research support.

Thank you to my beloved wife, Elisangela, and my two beautiful princesses, Liel and Hannah, who gave up their time with Papai over our summer vacation to let me work on this book. I love you very much.

And last, but certainly not least, I thank our faithful God, "the Keeper of Israel [who] neither slumbers nor sleeps" (Ps. 121:4).

INTRODUCTION

WHEN ISAIAH PROPHESIED the coming of the Messiah, he wrote: "He had no form or majesty that we should look at Him, nor beauty that we should desire Him" (53:2). In fact, the prophet went on to say, "He was despised and rejected by men" (Isa. 53:3). To the human eye, Yeshua (Jesus) seemed like an insignificant, ordinary man. He even came into the world in a lowly, drafty grotto rather than in a palace or even a clean room. Yet He was the Messiah, the Redeemer, the Holy One of Israel. Obviously, God's ways are different than ours!

In a similar way, the nation of Israel seems insignificant—a tiny country spread over a few thousand square miles of deserts and hills in the Middle East. Slightly bigger than the state of New Jersey, Israel is not the world's largest, richest, or most powerful nation. Yet in God's eyes it is by far the most important nation on Earth. This tiny people with their tiny land are the apple of God's eye, and because of this, the history of our entire planet is bound up with the history of Israel.

If you want to understand what God is doing in these last days, you must understand what He is doing with Israel. It is there that the Bible's prophecies regarding the end of the age will all unfold.

The Last Days Are Here

Everywhere I go, I hear people speculating about whether these might be the last days of planet Earth. People sense that we are heading toward a cataclysm. Even people who don't consider themselves to be religious are talking about it. There are many reasons this is true.

First of all, it's difficult to understand the hatred and complete disregard for human life that is the hallmark of radical jihadists and their sympathizers. Just think about what we've witnessed. Gunmen massacre innocent, unarmed civilians watching a concert.[1] A truck driver purposefully runs over dozens of people during a Bastille Day celebration in France, slaughtering innocent men, women, and children.[2] Here in the United States we have experienced massacres in San Bernardino, California; Orlando, Florida; and Boston, Massachusetts, among other cities. Elsewhere in the world there have been attacks in Paris, London, Istanbul—the list goes on. Just look at the death toll in Iraq, where it seems there is at least one suicide bombing every week. There have been so many mass killings, in fact, that it's difficult to remember them all. Before we've had time to grieve one bloody tragedy, the next one happens.

And then there are the unrelenting wars that continue throughout the Middle East. Civil war has left Syria in ruins and sent millions fleeing into Europe, causing a refugee crisis there—and resulting in the deaths of thousands of people who have drowned trying to cross the Mediterranean Sea into Europe.

And the bloodshed continues in Israel, where terror attacks are commonplace and rockets continue to rain down—fifteen thousand of them since 2001.[3] I could go on and on. There are the racial tensions and assassinations of white police officers here in the United States as well as renewed belligerence on the part of Russia and efforts to expand their control. For years we have fooled ourselves into thinking human beings are getting better—more civilized and humane. Now the ugly truth is out: we are the same old flawed humanity we have always been. The Bible is on the mark when it says:

> But understand this, that in the last days hard times will come—for people will be lovers of self, lovers of money, boastful, arrogant, blasphemers, disobedient to parents, ungrateful, unholy, hardhearted, unforgiving, backbiting, without self-control, brutal, hating what is good, treacherous, reckless, conceited, lovers of pleasure rather than lovers of God, holding to an outward form of godliness but denying its power. Avoid these people!
>
> —2 Timothy 3:1–5

Yes, the end of the age is near, but that is not a bad thing for those who belong to God and serve Him diligently. The end does not mean destruction for God's people but rather redemption and the emergence of a new chapter of history, one of peace and freedom from suffering. Despite the terrors we see all around us, God is still in control, and He has a plan to bring everything together for our good. As Yeshua Himself said, "Now when these things begin to happen, stand straight and lift up your heads, because your salvation is near!" (Luke 21:28).

Redemption Through Israel

The role of Israel, both the land and the people, is foundational to understanding God's redemptive plan for mankind. Since our first ancestors brought sin into the world in the Garden of Eden, God's divine plan to redeem us from sin and restore us into a relationship with Himself through His Anointed One, the Messiah, has been unfolding.

God's Son, the promised Redeemer of mankind, gave His life for our sins in Jerusalem almost two thousand years ago. It was there that He was crucified and buried, rose from the dead, and then ascended into heaven. It was in Jerusalem that God chose to have His temple built and to dwell among His people. It was in Israel that He performed great signs and wonders. And Jerusalem and Israel are where He will ultimately fulfill the words written by His prophets thousands of years ago.

You and I are privileged to be experiencing things today that the ancient prophets of Israel longed to see for themselves. I would not want to live in any other period because I know that God is bringing about the final wrap-up of history, and He has honored us by allowing us to be a part of it.

This book provides seven keys to understanding Israel's past, present, and future role in God's plan to recover a corrupt and lost world. His plan will culminate in the utter defeat of evil and all principalities and powers, and the establishment of a Messianic age of peace and prosperity.

I believe that just by reading this book you are saying, "I want to be part of what God is doing in these last days. I want to thoroughly understand the role of Israel and the Jewish people in this part of God's ultimate plan."

I also believe that God is calling you to read this book. You didn't pick it up by accident. He wants you to take the truths you learn within these pages and share them with others—to be salt and light to a church that, for the most part, does not understand how Israel ties into their salvation and the future redemption of the world. Just as Israel is experiencing a partial blindness that keeps them from recognizing Jesus as their Messiah, much of the church is walking in a partial blindness that keeps them from recognizing the role of Israel in God's plan for the redemption of the nations.

I am convinced that it is vital for the church to recognize these seven keys to unlocking and understanding end-times prophecy and to understand the role all believers play in the return of our Messiah and Savior, Yeshua (Jesus) of Nazareth.

Why Israel?

Before we enter into an in-depth discussion of Israel's role in these last days, I want to briefly touch on three reasons Israel plays such an important part in God's plans for the future of this planet.

1. The Bible tells us that in the end of the age, Jews will return to Israel from the nations of the world they were scattered to. This is happening right now. The prophet Ezekiel prophesied: "For thus says *Adonai Elohim*: 'Here I am! I Myself will search for My sheep and seek them out. As a shepherd seeks out his sheep on the day he is among his scattered flock, so I will seek out My sheep. I will rescue them out of all the places where they have been scattered, on a day of cloud and thick darkness. I will bring them out from the peoples. I will gather them from the countries. I will bring them back to their own land. I will shepherd them upon the mountains of Israel, by the streams and in all the habitable places of the land'" (Ezek. 34:11–13).

And Isaiah 11:10–12 says: "It will also come about in that day that the root of Jesse will stand as a banner for the peoples. The nations will seek for Him, and His resting place will be glorious. It will also come about in that day that my Lord will again redeem—a second time with His hand—the remnant of His people who remain from Assyria, from Egypt, from Pathros, from Cush, Elam, Shinar, Hamath, and from the islands of the sea. He will lift up a banner for the nations, and assemble the dispersed of Israel, and gather the scattered of Judah from the four corners of the earth."

2. God says that in the last days His Spirit will be poured out upon the Jewish people. This too is happening now, as thousands of Jews are coming to faith in the Messiah.

   The growth of Messianic Judaism has been incredible. In 1967, before the Jewish people regained control of Jerusalem, there were just a handful of Messianic congregations in the United States (then called Hebrew Christian congregations) and only several thousand Jewish believers in Jesus worldwide. Today there are more than eight hundred Messianic Jewish congregations in the United States and across the globe, with more than one hundred in Israel alone.[4]

   There are well over one hundred thousand Jews in the United States who express faith in Yeshua. Also, by some estimates, more than one hundred thousand Jewish people in the former Soviet Union have made professions of faith in Yeshua since the early 1990s.[5]

   Philip Yancey writes, "Despite two thousand years of the great divide, despite all that has taken place in this century of violent anti-Semitism, interest in Jesus is resurging among the Jews. In 1925, when the Hebrew scholar Joseph Klausner decided to write a book about Jesus, he could find only three full-length treatments of Jesus' life by contemporary Jewish scholars. Now there are hundreds, including some of the most illuminating studies available."[6]

3. When the Messiah comes again, He will return to Israel, where "they will look toward Me whom they pierced. They will mourn for him as one mourns for an only son and grieve bitterly for him, as one grieves for a firstborn" (Zech. 12:10).

A Word of Warning

Before we go further, I want to issue a note of caution that you might not expect to read in a book like this one: don't believe everything you hear about the end times. While I believe it is unmistakable that Bible prophecies are being fulfilled all around us, I also believe that the study of prophecy is fertile ground for false teachers and charlatans. Unfortunately, there is a great deal of inaccuracy and sensationalism mixed in with the truth. We must be like the Bereans, who "search[ed] the Scriptures each day to see whether these things were true" (Acts 17:11).

When I was just starting out in ministry, a visiting speaker came to the church where I was serving as an associate pastor in Rochester, New York, and told the people that construction was almost complete on the end-time temple in Jerusalem. He even had pictures to prove it. As you can imagine, a lot of people listening to him were excited about this. The problem was that it wasn't true and I knew it. Having lived in Israel while studying in college, I recognized the "new temple" in his photographs was a Conservative synagogue that had been erected a decade previously. I had to challenge this false teacher in his fancy suit because I knew he was not telling the truth, even though he insisted otherwise. God's people must be diligent and weigh all they hear carefully, at all times and in all situations. Everything must be measured against the Word of God and the facts.

There is a great deal of false and misleading information out there. Some of it is borne out of wishful thinking, and some of it out of a desire for personal gain. But if there is a counterfeit, there must also be a genuine article.

What is true is that a movement to rebuild the temple is underway. I have met and interviewed some of the leading figures. These Orthodox Jews passionately believe this must take place to usher in the Messiah. And it is also true that a Temple Institute now exists, and they are fashioning the furniture and articles necessary for a rebuilt temple. Beyond that, not much of what is being reported is accurate. This group still represents only a tiny minority of religious Jews in Israel. But the movement is growing.

Various sources, including Charisma News, have reported on the Temple Institute and other organizations that desire a rebuilt temple on the Temple Mount, where the Dome of the Rock currently stands. Charisma quotes my dear friend Jonathan Cahn, author of the best-selling book *The Harbinger*, as saying, "We know that end-time prophecy cannot be fulfilled without the rebuilding of the Temple in Jerusalem. The abomination desolation prophesied in Daniel and in the Gospels must take place within the Temple precincts. So, too, the apostle Paul speaks of the 'man of sin,' or the Antichrist, sitting in the Temple of God. What many people don't realize is that along with the Holy of Holies, the altar of the Temple is the most central and critical part of the Temple."[7]

So again, don't believe everything you hear. But don't be guilty of throwing the baby out with the bathwater. Even in the first century, Paul said that some people were preaching the good news of Yeshua's atoning death, burial, and resurrection simply because they thought they could make some money from doing so. But Paul said that even if the gospel was preached with poor motives, good could come out of it:

> The latter do so out of love, knowing that I am appointed for the defense of the Good News. The former proclaim Messiah not sincerely, but out of selfishness—expecting to stir up trouble for me in my imprisonment. But what does it matter? Only that in every way, whether in dishonesty or in truth, Messiah is being proclaimed—and in this I rejoice!
>
> —PHILIPPIANS 1:16–18

And despite the confusion that exists due to false teachers—and some others who insist on setting a date for His return, even though He Himself said His coming would be like a thief in the night and that not even He knew the date or hour of His return—Yeshua said that He expects us to be ready for and expecting His return.

> Therefore stay alert; for you do not know what day your Lord is coming. But know this, that if the master of the house had known what time the thief was coming, he would have kept watch and not let his house be broken into. So you also must be ready, for the Son of Man is coming at an hour you do not expect.
>
> —MATTHEW 24:42–44

The prophet Daniel also said that the wise would understand when the last days of planet Earth were drawing near:

> Then I, Daniel, looked and behold, two others stood there, one on this bank of the river and the one on the other bank of the river. One said to the man clothed in linen, who was above the waters of the river, "How long until the end of the wondrous things?"
>
> Then I heard the man clothed in linen, who was above the waters of the river, as he raised both his right and left hands toward heaven and swore an oath by Him who lives forever, saying, "It is for a time, times, and a half. Then when the breaking of the power of the holy people comes to an end, all these things will be finished."
>
> Now I heard, but I did not understand. So I said, "My Lord, what will be the outcome of these things?"
>
> Then he said: "Go your way, Daniel. For the words are closed up and sealed until the time of the end. Many will be purified, made spotless and refined, but the wicked will act wickedly. None of the wicked will understand, but the wise will understand."
>
> —Daniel 12:5–10

Two Sides of the Messiah

Now, I admit that anyone who reads what the Hebrew Scriptures have to say about the Messiah may wind up a bit confused. In some passages He is presented as the great conqueror who will wage war on His enemies and avenge His people. These references are related to His kingship. In others He is presented as a meek and humble servant who would be rejected, suffer, and die. These references are related to His servanthood. How can these apparently contradictory prophecies of the Messiah be reconciled?

Could it be that there are two Messiahs? The ancient sages of Israel thought so. They believed the first, Messiah ben Yosef (son of Joseph), would be rejected by his brothers as was Joseph, the son of

Rachel, who was sold into slavery but later rose to save his family from starvation. The second, Messiah ben David, would restore the golden age to Israel and, like his forefather David, would rule and reign over a kingdom of peace and abundance.

Actually, they weren't that far off. But rather than two Messiahs, each coming once, we now know from the revelation of the New Testament that the Old Testament Scriptures prophesied one Messiah coming twice!

The first time the Messiah appeared on Earth, He came as a lowly servant born in a drafty cave. When He comes again, "He is coming with the clouds, and every eye shall see him" (Rev. 1:7).

When Yeshua was born into this world two thousand years ago, He came as the Suffering Servant foretold by the prophet Isaiah:

> Who has believed our report? To whom is the arm of *Adonai* revealed? For He grew up before Him like a tender shoot, like a root out of dry ground. He had no form or majesty that we should look at Him, nor beauty that we should desire Him. He was despised and rejected by men, a man of sorrows, acquainted with grief, One from whom people hide their faces. He was despised, and we did not esteem Him. Surely He has borne our griefs and carried our pains. Yet we esteemed Him stricken, struck by God, and afflicted. But He was pierced because of our transgressions, crushed because of our iniquities. The chastisement for our *shalom* was upon Him, and by His stripes we are healed. We all like sheep have gone astray. Each of us turned to his own way. So *Adonai* has laid on Him the iniquity of us all. He was oppressed and He was afflicted yet He did not open His mouth. Like a lamb led to the slaughter, like a sheep before its shearers is silent, so He did not open His mouth.
>
> —Isaiah 53:1–7

The Book of Revelation paints a completely different picture of the Messiah's return:

> Then I saw heaven opened, and behold, a white horse! The One riding on it is called Faithful and True, and He judges and makes war in righteousness. His eyes are like a flame of fire, and many royal crowns are on His head.... And the armies of heaven, clothed in fine linen, white and clean, were following Him on white horses. From His mouth comes a sharp sword—so that with it He may strike down the nations—and He shall rule them with an iron rod, and He treads the winepress of the furious wrath of *Elohei-Tzva'ot*. On His robe and on His thigh He has a name written, "King of kings, and Lord of lords."
>
> —Revelation 19:11–12, 14–16

You can know for certain that the Messiah is coming again, not as the Suffering Servant but as the great King of kings and Lord of lords who will vanquish evil and rule over all nations. And He calls us to be watching, waiting, and ready for His return.

Before we move on to a discussion of the first of the seven keys to unlocking the prophetic mysteries of Israel, please pray this prayer with me:

> *Thank You, Lord, for this opportunity to discover Your great mysteries regarding Israel and the Jewish people. Please develop in me a heart for Your people, Israel. Give me Your heart. Use me, Lord, to advance Your kingdom and bless the Jewish people according to Your promise that You will bless those who bless Israel* (Gen. 12:3). *In the mighty name of Yeshua, Jesus, who died and rose again, amen.*

Chapter 1

KEY ONE: THE SEED PROMISE

> ADONAI *Elohim* said to the serpent, "Because you did this, cursed are you above all the livestock and above every animal of the field. On your belly will you go, and dust will you eat all the days of your life. I will put animosity between you and the woman—between your seed and her seed. He will crush your head, and you will crush his heel."
>
> —GENESIS 3:14–15

WE'VE ALL SEEN the chilling photographs. Rows of emaciated prisoners in ragged, striped pajamas with arms and legs the size of fragile twigs. They look out at the world through sunken, lifeless eyes that have experienced unbelievable horror. They appear to be only days away from death by starvation.

These are the survivors of Nazi concentration camps that were set up to deal with "the Jewish problem" during World War II. The photographs were taken as they were rescued by the Allies during the closing days of the war.

What crime had these prisoners committed? Nothing—except that they were Jews. Because of this, and this alone, they were arrested and subjected to unbelievable abuse and torture. Six million of them died and many were reduced to ashes in Nazi ovens.

Nazi butchery of the Jews is difficult to explain or understand. There was a savagery to it that defies belief. The hatred was so deep that I believe there was a supernatural aspect to it.

Just consider these words from Adolf Hitler and two of his top officials:

> ...the personification of the devil as the symbol of all evil assumes the living shape of the Jew.[1]
>
> —ADOLF HITLER

> I believe that I am acting in accordance with the will of the Almighty Creator: by defending myself against the Jew, I am fighting for the work of the Lord.[2]
>
> —ADOLF HITLER

> The Führer once more expressed his determination to clean up the Jews in Europe pitilessly. There must be no squeamish sentimentalism about it. The Jews have deserved the catastrophe that has now overtaken them. Their destruction will now go hand in hand with the destruction of our enemies. We must hasten this process with cold ruthlessness.[3]
>
> —JOSEPH GOEBBELS,
> REICH PROPAGANDA MINISTER

> One way or another—I will tell you quite openly—we must finish off the Jews....Gentlemen, I must ask you to steel

> yourselves against all considerations of compassion. We must destroy the Jews wherever we find them, and wherever it is at all possible.[4]
>
> —Hans Frank,
> Governor of Occupied Poland

The first key to unlocking the prophetic mysteries of Israel is to understand that Satan hates the Jews with a furious passion and will do anything to destroy them.

Why does Satan hate the Jews so deeply? It's because he knows something most Christians don't—that God's plan to redeem this world comes through the Jews. It did in the beginning, and it is still the case today. Our redemption—our victory—is the enemy's defeat. And as the time for our victory comes closer, he is becoming increasingly determined in his effort to destroy the Jews.

Not long ago I came across a photograph from the dark days of the Third Reich that I can't get out of my mind. It's a picture of a young girl of perhaps twelve or thirteen standing in the middle of a field on a clear winter's day. She has a look of terror on her face. Her body is contorted as if she wants to run but doesn't know which way to go. We are looking at her from behind a Nazi machine gunner who has her in his sights. My assumption is that this innocent child was shot down an instant after the photograph was taken.

Of course, the gunner would say that he was just "following orders." But how could he possibly do such a thing, no matter what he had been told to do or who had told him to do it? How could he be so hateful and callous that he would not defy those orders, even though to do so would most certainly mean the end of his own life?

"The Haters Are Still Here"

Elie Wiesel, the Nobel Prize–winning author and Holocaust survivor, passed away just as I began to write this book. Wiesel was interred in Auschwitz when he was just fifteen years old. His mother and sister were killed the first night. His father died in Buchenwald shortly before it was liberated. In an interview with his old friend Georg Klein—a renowned Jewish biologist who escaped Auschwitz only by running away when the Nazis attempted to force him onto a train bound for the death camp—Wiesel said:

> I was convinced that hatred among nations and among people perished in Auschwitz. It didn't. The victims died but the haters are still here. New ones. And so often I say to myself, "Really, what are we doing on this planet?" We are passing the message as well as we can, communicating our fears, our hopes...Day in day out, week after week and year after year, people kill each other.[5]

Wiesel endured so much. Yet when Klein asked him about his faith in God, he replied, "I come from a very religious background....And actually I remained in it. All my anger I describe in my quarrels with God in Auschwitz, but you know I used to pray every day....My faith is a wounded faith, but...my life is not without faith. I didn't divorce God, but I'm quarrelling and arguing and questioning, it's a wounded faith."[6]

A History of Hatred

There has never been a race of people as hated as the Jews. It didn't begin with Hitler nor did it end there. Even people considered to be among America's greatest heroes have said terrible things about the Jews. The great industrialist Henry Ford said, "Jews have actually invaded, in person and in program, hundreds of American churches, with their subversive and impossible social ideals, and at last became so cocksure of their domination of the situation that they were met with the inevitable check."[7]

He also said, "Abraham was not a Jew; Isaac was not a Jew… Samuel was not a Jew; even Esther and Mordecai were not Jews, but Benjaminites; the majority of the prophets were not Jews, but Israelites."[8] This sort of thinking is propagated today in dozens of publications and websites. Even though the Holocaust is one of history's most thoroughly documented occurrences, some insist it never happened. They say it was a hoax, perpetrated by Jews. I've even heard it suggested that the Holocaust was actually perpetrated by the Jews against ordinary German citizens. In other words, they believe Germany's Jews gassed and machine-gunned six million Germans and then turned things around to make it look as if they were the victims. It amazes me to see the lengths to which hatred will go to justify itself. Just a quick visit online revealed dozens of websites claiming the Holocaust is a complete hoax.

Some of these people even use the words of Jesus to justify their hatred of the Jews. John 8:44 is one their favorite verses: "You are of your father the devil, and you want to do the desires of your father. He was a murderer from the beginning and does not stand in the truth, because there is no truth in him. Whenever he speaks lies he is just being himself—for he is a liar and the father of lies."

These are harsh words, but they are not aimed at the Jewish people as a whole but rather at a specific group of leaders who refused to believe that Yeshua had been sent by God and were seeking to undermine Him out of pride and arrogance. Yeshua's love for His own brethren shines throughout the Scriptures. It was the Jews He preached to, healed, and raised from the dead. When

He pronounced the blessings of the Beatitudes, He was speaking to Jewish people.

When Jesus sent His disciples to drive out evil spirits and heal the sick, He told them, "Do not go to the Gentiles, and do not enter into any Samaritan town. But go instead to the lost sheep of the house of Israel" (Matt. 10:5–6). In Matthew 15, when a Canaanite woman came begging Jesus to heal her daughter, He replied that He was sent only to the lost sheep of Israel. (Of course, He did heal the little girl, as we would expect of Him.) And when He was on His way to be crucified, the Bible tells us that He wept over Jerusalem (Luke 19:41).

These are not the actions of someone who hated the Jews. As the apostle Paul wrote to the believers at Rome:

> Then what is the advantage of being Jewish? Or what is the benefit of circumcision? Much in every way. First of all, they were entrusted with the sayings of God. So what if some did not trust? Will their lack of faith nullify God's faithfulness? May it never be! Let God be true even if every man is a liar, as it is written, "that You may be righteous in Your words and prevail when You are judged."
>
> —Romans 3:1–4

Why do people hate the Jews so much? The answer is simple. They hate the Jews because Satan hates the Jews, and he has put it into their hearts. And Satan hates the Jews because God has chosen them to be the means through which He brings about the redemption of mankind.

It's amazing what seemingly intelligent, well-educated people will say about the Jews when they let their guard down. Have you ever heard someone say about the Jews, "They're all stingy money-grubbers"? I have. And yet many of the Jewish people I know are among the kindest, most selfless and giving people on earth. So how did the Jews come to be thought of as cheap and miserly?

Long ago, Jews were not permitted to go into many trades that were controlled by Christians due to anti-Semitism, so they found themselves in professions that were unattractive to Christians. Because of the way Scripture was interpreted at the time, Christians weren't allowed to charge interest on loans, so handling money was considered a despicable profession for Christians. Thus many Jews became moneylenders. Over time they got very good at banking and lending, and many became quite wealthy. This caused some to become jealous and resentful of the Jews in general, which led to the erroneous stereotype.[9]

Another falsehood I've heard is, "The Jews own all the media and they lie to us about everything." Or, "All the big banks are run by Jews...and they're out to rip us off any way they can." There is a joke I love to tell. Shlomi is on the subway and sees his friend Moishe reading an anti-Semitic newspaper. He can ignore it no longer and decides to confront him. "Moishe, you're a Jew. How can you read a horrible paper like that?"

"Easy," Moishe replies. "When I read the *New York Times,* all I read is that Jews are being shot; Jewish cemeteries are being desecrated; our synagogues are being bombed. But when I read this paper it says Jews own all the banks; Jews run the media; Jews are taking over the world. The news they are reporting in this paper is so much better!"

In truth, most of the Jewish people I know (and I know a lot) are just ordinary people who work hard, try to be good humans, and want the best for the communities they live in. How did they come to be pictured as misers and villains who keep the rest of us under their control?

I didn't know much about anti-Semitism when I was a boy

growing up in upstate New York. Most of the kids I hung out with were Christians—at least insofar as their church affiliation went. I can't really remember anyone putting me down because I was Jewish. I first came face-to-face with unreasoning hatred of the Jews when I visited Moscow in the early 1990s. I was with a group of other Jewish believers in Jesus who were putting on a street performance and then handing out invitations to attend a large festival we were hosting in that city.

People seemed to like what we were doing until they read the invitation and realized we were Messianic Jews. "Jews, go home!" some began to shout. Others surged forward in a threatening manner, shaking their fists and spitting at us.

Many of our attackers were gray-haired elders, grandmothers and grandfathers. Not the sort of people you would expect to see getting involved in a brawl or attacking strangers. It shook me to see how their faces were twisted by hate as soon as they discovered we were Jews. It was like watching Dr. Jekyll drink the potion that turned him into Mr. Hyde.

One elderly woman screamed, "I hate Jews! You should all burn in hell for what you have done!" Someone else shouted, "You Jews are pigs! Devils!" Another tore up the flyer she had been given, threw it on the ground, and began spitting on it. Shouts of "*Heil* Hitler" were heard, and some members of our group were physically assaulted. Thanks to God, no one was injured seriously.

On another occasion, in London, I encountered a group of people protesting against Israel. Because I wanted to see what the literature they were handing out contained, I went over and took one of their brochures. I wasn't surprised to discover that in addition to anti-Zionist propaganda they were distributing lies about the Jewish people that came directly from the fraudulent and malicious book *The Protocols of the Elders of Zion*. I asked them why they were spreading lies about the Jews, though I already knew the answer. The root of the problem is spiritual.

The Protocols of the Elders of Zion was first published over one hundred years ago. It accuses the Jewish people of all sorts of despicable things. The Jewish Virtual Library calls the *Protocols* "the most notorious and most successful work of modern anti-Semitism."[10] The Virtual Library goes on to explain that the *Protocols*

> draws on popular anti-Semitic notions which have their roots in medieval Europe from the time of the Crusades. The libels that the Jews used blood of Christian children for the Feast of Passover, poisoned the wells and spread the plague were pretexts for the wholesale destruction of Jewish communities throughout Europe. Tales were circulated among the masses of secret rabbinical conferences whose aim was to subjugate and exterminate the Christians, and motifs like these are found in early anti-Semitic literature.... In the civil war following the Bolshevik Revolution of 1917, the reactionary White Armies made extensive use of the Protocols to incite widespread slaughters of Jews.[11]

The *Protocols* actually date back to a late 1700s book that blamed the Freemasons for the slaughter that took place during the French Revolution. In later editions the Masons were replaced by the Jews, and the text was broadened beyond what had taken place in France. Even though the book was proved beyond any doubt to be a forgery, it "formed an important part of the Nazis' justification of genocide of the Jews in the Holocaust."[12] I recently read that the *Protocols* is a best seller again in Russia even though the book has been proved again and again to be nothing more than a libelous fraud.

Perhaps even more troubling than the *Protocols* is that many of the great Christian leaders and theologians since the third century have promulgated anti-Semitism within the church. Consider the great Protestant leader Martin Luther. When he first began to preach, Luther loved the Jewish people and recognized them as God's chosen people. He also believed they would eventually respond to the gospel and believe in Jesus. But when this didn't happen, he apparently turned against them and became bitter. Here is just a small portion of what Luther wrote in his book *On the Jews and Their Lies*:

> What shall we Christians do with this rejected and condemned people, the Jews? Since they live among us, we dare not tolerate their conduct, now that we are aware of their lying and reviling and blaspheming. If we do, we become sharers in their lies, cursing and blasphemy....I shall give you my sincere advice:
>
> First, to set fire to their synagogues or schools and to bury and cover with dirt whatever will not burn, so that no man will ever again see a stone or cinder of them. This is to be done in honor of our Lord and of Christendom, so that God might see that we are Christians, and do not condone or knowingly tolerate such public lying, cursing, and blaspheming of his Son and of his Christians....
>
> Second, I advise that their houses also be razed and destroyed. For they pursue in them the same aims as in their synagogues. Instead they might be lodged under a roof or in a barn, like the gypsies. This will bring home to them the fact that they are not masters in our country, as they boast, but that they are living in exile and in captivity, as they incessantly wail and lament about us before God.
>
> Third, I advise that all their prayer books and Talmudic writings, in which such idolatry, lies, cursing, and blasphemy are taught, be taken from them.[13]

Although Luther was a great reformer, he also paved the way theologically for Hitler and the Nazis to carry out their genocide against the Jews. Because of teachers such as Luther, sadly many "good Christians" thought they were doing "God's work."

Anti-Semitism has existed since the Israelites were slaves in Egypt and has continually plagued the descendants of Abraham, Isaac, and Jacob. Alarmingly, this hatred toward the Jews is on the rise again everywhere. Jewish Voice Ministries has experienced such anti-Semitic hatred. A few years ago our offices were visited by local and federal agents and members of Homeland Security after we received a serious cyber threat. All of our computer hard drives were taken, and the investigators told us to take the threat very seriously.

The story is the same all over the world. Anti-Defamation League National Director Abraham Foxman stated in 2015 that anti-Semitism had reached its highest level since World War II.[14] Jewish men, women, and children have been attacked without provocation. Synagogues have been vandalized. Graveyards have been desecrated, Holocaust memorials destroyed, and houses painted with swastikas and vulgar messages.[15]

During the five years between 1997 and 2002, there were 1,127 violent attacks against Jews around the world. In the following five years, from 2003 to 2008, that number nearly tripled to 3,051 attacks. Between 2009 and 2014, that number jumped again to 4,264.[16]

As you can see, the situation is not getting better, but worse. The statistics are more than tragic. They are a sign that Satan is lashing out with more urgency as the date of our Messiah's return, and thus the end of the current age, draws closer.

WHERE DOES THE HATRED COME FROM?

This hatred of the Jews has its roots in man's fall from grace thousands of years ago, with a curse pronounced in the Garden of Eden. In Genesis chapter 3, God pronounces a curse upon Satan, who has brought sin into the world by deceiving Adam and Eve to eat the fruit from the tree of the knowledge of good and evil even though God had specifically forbidden them from doing so. God tells Satan, who has come to the first humans in the form of a serpent:

> I will put animosity between you and the woman—between your seed and her seed. He will crush your head, and you will crush his heel.
>
> —GENESIS 3:15

Bible scholars refer to this verse as the protevangelium, the "pre-gospel," or the first of the Bible's prophecies of a coming redeemer. God is declaring, in essence, a redeemer will be born into the world through the seed of the woman (the descendant of Eve)—and although you will do your best to destroy Him, you will only be able to inflict an injury on His heel. He will then crush your head, or utterly destroy you.

As I pointed out in my book *A Rabbi Looks at the Last Days*, the ancient Jewish sages once interpreted this verse as a prophecy about the coming of Messiah. In addition, the verse also reveals that the Messiah would be the child of a virgin. Note the verse states "her seed" and not "his seed," which would be expected since seed is always related to a man. In fact, when the Hebrew Scriptures were later translated into Greek around 250 BC (that document became known as the Septuagint, or LXX), the Jewish translators replaced the Hebrew word used in Genesis 3:15, *zera`* (זֶרַע), with the Greek word *sperma*, from which we derive the word *sperm*. In other words, the verse is saying "the sperm of the woman." Without the idea of a virgin birth this wording makes no sense.

The concept of a virgin birth is repeated in Isaiah 7:14: "The virgin shall conceive, and bear a son, and shall call his name Immanuel" (MEV). We know this was fulfilled with the coming of Yeshua, born of a virgin.

Since that historic moment in the Garden of Eden, Satan has known that his days are numbered. He has been sentenced to death but is doing everything within his power to keep that sentence from being carried out. He is like a dangerous criminal who is out of prison on bail while his attorney files one appeal after another. In the meantime, he is continuing to wreak havoc on those who get within striking distance. And although God Almighty, the great Judge of the universe, has sentenced the serpent, Satan, to death, that great deceiver has deceived himself into believing he can avoid his punishment. But he won't.

Now, Satan wasn't the only one who understood the prophecy in Genesis 3:15. Adam and Eve understood that a child was going to be born into the world who would crush the head of the serpent—and they also believed that when that day came, God would allow them back into the garden. They had the general idea right, but they were off by a few thousand years.

Adam and Eve desperately wanted to get back into that garden, where life had been so easy and beautiful and they talked face-to-face with God every day. In the garden there were no sore throats, no headaches, no upset stomachs, no pain of any kind. There was no dust, no anxiety, no sweat or hard labor for food—just day after day of bliss.

I believe they talked a lot about seeing the promise fulfilled because they wanted to get back into paradise. When their first son, Cain, was born, I'm certain they believed he would be the one to defeat the serpent who had deceived them. The Bible says that when Cain was born, Eve said, "I have gotten a man from the LORD" (Gen. 4:1, KJV), or as the Tree of Life translation says, "I produced a man with *ADONAI*."

If we go back to the original Hebrew, the literal translation can read, "I have gotten a son, the Lord"—in other words, a child who is the Lord. The idea here is that Adam and Eve may well have thought Cain was the promised redeemer who would make everything right and grant them access back into the Garden of Eden.

Tragically, this is not what happened. Cain was born into a world now corrupted by sin. His parents likely believed he was going to grow up to be the redeemer, the one who would finally crush the head of the serpent and restore things to God's original design. But instead he became a murderer who killed his own brother. Talk about heartbreak and disappointment.

Cain's story illustrates the terrible things that have come into the world through sin. Sin does more than cause a few weeds and thorns to grow. Sin brought about a radical transformation of the world that resulted in hate, murder, war, and all the violence and terror we see today. Sin resulted in death, decay, and destruction—and we are still living in the aftermath of this terrible transformation.

Let's jump now to Genesis chapter 12, where we read about another "seed promise."

> My heart's desire is to make you into a great nation, to bless you, to make your name great so that you may be a blessing. My desire is to bless those who bless you, but whoever curses you I will curse, and in you all the families of the earth will be blessed.
>
> —GENESIS 12:2–3

We'll talk much more about this passage in the next chapter. For now, I just want to say that these verses contain another Messianic prophecy, this time that the redeemer would come through the line of Abraham. Satan, who hates us and wants to keep us in bondage to him, understood these prophecies and wanted to do everything he could to prevent them from happening. Because he understood the role God destined Abraham's descendants—or even more specifically, his descendant—to play in the redemption of the world, Satan has continually tried to destroy the Jewish people. After all, if he could wipe the Jewish race off the face of the earth, then the prophecies about a coming Messiah and Savior could never come true.

He first tried to destroy the Israelites when they were slaves in Egypt. Although the children of Israel were abused and mistreated, Pharaoh saw that they were strong and growing stronger. It is likely that their birth rate was much higher than that of their Egyptian neighbors, and Pharaoh was also aware they were ripe for rebellion and crying out to their God for a deliverer. Fearing they would soon be strong enough to rebel, he decided to prevent this by killing every baby boy born to a Hebrew family (Exod. 1:22).

If the plan had succeeded, the Hebrew race would have eventually been wiped out, as there would have been no men for the young women to marry. But God had other plans. Moses's mother hid him from the king's execution squads, and he grew up right under Pharaoh's nose to be a mighty deliverer who led his people out of bondage in Egypt.

Satan's next attempt to destroy the Jews came nearly a thousand years later when a government official named Haman became so enraged over a Jewish man's refusal to show him proper respect that he decided to try to have the entire race murdered. Haman's plotting against the Jews is revealed in the third chapter of the Book of Esther:

> When Haman saw that Mordecai was not bowing down or paying him honor, Haman was filled with rage. But it was repugnant in his eyes to lay hands on Mordecai alone, for they had told him the identity of Mordecai's people. So Haman sought to destroy all the Jews, the people of Mordecai, who were throughout the whole kingdom of Ahasuerus....
>
> Haman then said to King Ahasuerus: "There is a certain people scattered and dispersed among the peoples in all the provinces of your kingdom whose laws differ from those of every other people and who do not obey the king's laws. It is not in the king's interest to tolerate them. If it pleases the king, let an edict be written to destroy them. I will pay 10,000 talents of silver into the hands of those who carry out this business, to put it into the king's treasuries."
>
> The king took his signet ring from his hand and gave it to Haman—son of Hammedatha the Agagite—enemy of the Jews. The king said to Haman, "The silver and the people are yours—do with them as you please."
>
> —Esther 3:5–11

Haman also built the gallows upon which Mordecai was to be hanged. But his plans were thwarted by a beautiful Jewish queen named Esther. The Jewish people were spared, and Haman was executed on the gallows he had constructed for Mordecai.

Five centuries later, Satan used another king, Herod, to try to keep the Messiah from coming into the world. After Yeshua was born in Bethlehem, Herod ordered the killing of all boys there under the age of two. What the king didn't know was that Joseph,

Mary, and their child had already escaped into Egypt after an angel had warned them about the king's evil plan.

The next attempt came when Yeshua was arrested, falsely accused of crimes, and sentenced to die. I'm sure the devil was beside himself with glee. He didn't know that this was all part of God's plan. God's one and only Son was shedding His blood to open the gates of heaven to all mankind. The sins Adam and Eve committed had resulted in mankind being thrown out of paradise and separated from God. Yeshua gave His life as the second Adam so we could be restored to intimate fellowship with God.

But evil was not completely destroyed when Yeshua rose from the dead and ascended into heaven. As we've already seen, evil is rampant here in the twenty-first century. It is only when the Messiah returns to Earth and slays all His enemies that evil will disappear from the scene. Satan knows his time is short, and he is doing everything within his power to keep our Messiah from returning. He is like a panicked snake trapped in a corner, striking out in all directions, trying to inflict as much damage as he can so he can escape the judgment that has been pronounced against him.

The enemy knows that Israel plays a major role in God's plan to redeem mankind, so he is trying to destroy all the physical descendants of Abraham, Isaac, and Jacob. Satan knows the Bible, probably better than most of us. The Book of Matthew says that after Yeshua was baptized, He went into the wilderness, where the devil quoted Scripture in an attempt to persuade Him to abandon His plan to give His life for mankind. Satan knows every one of the Bible's prophecies, and he is trying to prevent them from becoming a reality. For example, the Bible says that in the last days Jews who have been scattered throughout the world will be gathered back to their land physically and then back to their God spiritually. We are seeing this happen before our very eyes. But Satan knows that if he can prevent this, the death sentence that hangs over his head will never be carried out. Make no mistake about it, Satan doesn't have an ounce of goodness in him. If he could save his own life by destroying every other living creature, he would. There is no doubt in my mind that this is true.

In fact, he has been trying to destroy the people of Israel for centuries. There has never been a time when the Jewish people have not been victimized by Satan's savage attacks against them. Here is a sampling of what the Jewish people have endured:

- AD 70—As many as one million Jews die during the revolt against Rome that culminates with the Roman army destroying the temple and burning the city of Jerusalem.[17]
- AD 135—The Romans crush the final revolt of the Jews, known as the Bar Kokhba revolt. Approximately 580,000 Jews are killed, and 50 fortified towns and 985 villages are razed.[18]
- AD 306—The Council of Elvira forbids Christians and Jews from intermarrying or eating together.[19]
- AD 413—A group of monks destroys synagogues and kills Jews as they travel through Palestine.[20]
- AD 1096—Thousands of Jews are massacred during the First Crusade, leaving dozens of Jewish cities entirely destroyed. The Jewish chronicler reports: "The enemies stripped them naked and dragged them off, granting quarter to none, save those few who accepted baptism."[21]

- AD 1182—Jews are expelled from France.[22]
- AD 1289—The Council of Vienna orders Jews to wear a round patch on their clothing.[23]
- AD 1290—Jews are expelled from England and southern Italy.[24]
- AD 1294—Jews are expelled from Bern, Switzerland.[25]
- AD 1347—Thousands of Jews are massacred after a rumor spreads that they started the Black Death by placing poison in wells.[26]
- AD 1475—All Jews in the city of Trent in Northern Italy are massacred after a rumor spreads that they have murdered a Christian boy for religious purposes.[27]
- AD 1492—The Jews are expelled from Spain.[28]
- AD 1497—Jews are expelled from Portugal.[29]
- AD 1826—Pope Leo XII issues a decree that Jews' property is to be confiscated and they are to live in ghettos.[30]

The list of what the Jewish people have suffered could go on for pages and fill an entire book. But despite these horrible injustices, and even though the country of Israel disappeared from the world map for a season, the Jewish people maintained their identity. They did so despite threats by despots like Pharaoh, Herod, and—possibly the worst of them all—Adolf Hitler.

And the hatred continues unabated. According to the website "Why Do People Hate the Jews?" more than 1.09 billion people in the world today have anti-Semitic attitudes.[31] The website also claims:

- one in three people believe the Holocaust never happened;
- during the last decade 60,822 anti-Semitic acts have taken place, more than 12,000 of them in the United States;
- seventeen acts of hatred against Jews are committed every day;
- 75 percent of Jewish students in the United States have experienced or witnessed anti-Semitic acts on campus;
- a survey conducted in nineteen countries revealed that 38 percent of people believe the Jews have too much power in business, and 15 percent believe the Jews are responsible for most wars.[32]

Please understand that I'm not blaming anyone for this or pointing fingers at any particular race or religion. Although it is obviously true that certain segments of the Christian church have been guilty of persecuting the Jews, anti-Semitic behavior did not start with the church. Nor did it originate with the Muslim religion, the Arabic people in general, or with the Nazis.

Satan and his hatred of God and His Word lies at the root of it all! He is the one who hates the Jews and will do anything within his power to destroy them. He is the one who has caused so much strife among brothers, which is what we really are. Our fault comes when we open our ears to his lies and allow him to seduce us, as Adam and Eve did in the Garden of Eden. The devil loves it when we refuse to see people as individuals, created in the image of God, but rather merely as members of a larger group we don't like. I doubt the Nazis ever thought about the fact that they were killing fathers and mothers, sons and children, husbands and wives—people who went to work every day to support their families, people who loved and laughed and cried and did all the things people do. As far as they were concerned, they were killing Jews. Nothing more.

Best-selling Christian author Philip Yancey speaks to this when he asks, "Is it possible to read the Gospels without blinders on? Jews read with suspicion, preparing to be scandalized. Christians read through the refracted lenses of church history. Both groups, I believe, would do well to pause and reflect on Matthew's first words, 'A record of the genealogy of Jesus Christ, son of David, son of Abraham.' The son of David speaks of Jesus' messianic line, which Jews should not ignore; 'a title which he would not deny to save his life cannot have been without significance for him,' notes C. H. Dodd. The son of Abraham speaks of Jesus' Jewish line, which we Christians dare not ignore either."[33]

He goes on to quote Yale University historian Jaroslav Pelikan: "Would there have been such anti-Semitism, would there have been so many pogroms, would there have been an Auschwitz, if every Christian church and every Christian home had focused its devotion and icons of Mary not only as Mother of God and Queen of heaven but as the Jewish maiden and the new Miriam, and on icons of Christ not only as a Pantocrator but as *Rabbi Jeshua bar-Joseph*, Rabbi Jesus of Nazareth?"[34]

Making Sense of It All

Some people look at what the Jewish people have endured, at the hatred directed at them, and say it makes no sense. But as we've seen, it makes absolute sense if we realize we have a supernatural enemy who wants to destroy us, and the very best way he can do that is to destroy the Jews.

Many "antichrists" have emerged throughout history. They all had the same goal—to destroy the children of Abraham, to wipe the Jewish race off the planet. Three, however, have been unique: Pharaoh, Herod, and Hitler. Each of these three appeared on the scene right before a great redemptive act of God. Pharaoh emerged before the Jews' exodus from Egypt and return to the Promised Land. Herod rose to power before the coming of the Messiah. And finally, Adolf Hitler emerged right before the regathering of the Jewish people back to their land after almost two thousand years and the reestablishment of the State of Israel as their homeland.

Do you see a pattern here? Satan knows exactly what he is doing and is able to discern the seasons of God's redemptive acts. He understands the times, and he knows the Jewish people are the key. His hope is that if he can destroy the Jews, he can destroy God's eternal plan of redemption. But as so many have discovered throughout world history, destroying the Jewish people is not an easy thing to do. As Mark Twain wrote in his article "Concerning the Jews":

> The Jews constitute but one percent of the human race.... Properly the Jew ought hardly to be heard of, but he is heard of, has always been heard of.... The Egyptian, the Babylonian, and the Persian rose, filled the planet with sound and splendor, then faded to dream-stuff and passed away; the Greek and the Roman followed, and made a vast noise, and they are gone; other people have sprung up and held their torch high for a time, but it burned out... The Jew saw them all, beat them all, and is now what he always was, exhibiting no decadence, no infirmities of age, no weakening of his parts, no slowing of his energies... All

> things are mortal, but the Jew; all other forces pass, but he remains. What is the secret of his immortality?[35]

The answer to this rhetorical question is abundantly clear. The secret of the Jew's immortality is that almighty God has chosen, blessed, and set him aside for a special purpose. It was through the Jewish people that the Messiah came into the world the first time, and they also will play a prominent role in His return. But more on that later.

The reason the Jewish people have endured despite countless efforts to eradicate them throughout history is because God, the Creator of the universe, has decreed their survival. Nowhere in Scripture is this decree clearer than in Jeremiah 31:34–36:

> Thus says *Adonai*, who gives the sun as a light by day and the fixed order of the moon and the stars as a light by night, who stirs up the sea so its waves roar, *Adonai-Tzva'ot* is His Name: "Only if this fixed order departs from before Me"—it is a declaration of *Adonai*—"then also might Israel's offspring cease from being a nation before Me—for all time." Thus says *Adonai*: "Only if heaven above can be measured and the foundations of the earth searched out beneath, then also I will cast off the offspring of Israel—for all they have done." It is a declaration of *Adonai*.

The previous verses make it crystal clear that despite Israel's rebellion and disobedience, they remain God's chosen nation. He will not allow them to disappear, nor will He replace them with another people as the erroneous doctrine of replacement theology teaches. If not for this decree, the Israelites—like the Canaanites, Jebusites, Amalekites, and all the other "-ites" of history—would have faded into antiquity.

In summary, in order to correctly understand the prophetic

mysteries yet to be fulfilled, we must first understand what has already taken place and why.

- A death sentence has been decreed over the serpent, Satan, and it will come to pass at some point in the future.
- Satan has deceived himself into believing he can circumvent this sentence from being carried out. How? By keeping the seed of the woman referenced in Genesis 3:15 from coming forth.
- Because he knows the Scriptures, Satan understands that this seed of the woman would come from the offspring of Abraham.
- Satan's efforts to destroy the children of Abraham throughout history is a logical and strategic effort to keep the death sentence pronounced over him from occurring.
- When we understand this, we understand that anti-Semitism is not some illogical hatred of Jews, but the evil one's systematic and calculated attempt at self-preservation.

So, the first key to understanding the role of Israel in end-time prophecy hinges on the logic that Satan understands that God is not finished with the Jewish people and that they will play a key role in what is yet to come. This is why we again see anti-Semitism on the rise and why Satan is so focused on the destruction of the Jews. But he cannot succeed, in part because of the second prophetic key: the Abrahamic blessing.

Chapter 2

KEY TWO: THE ABRAHAMIC BLESSING

> Get going out from your land, and from your relatives, and from your father's house, to the land that I will show you. My heart's desire is to make you into a great nation, to bless you, to make your name great so that you may be a blessing. My desire is to bless those who bless you, but whoever curses you I will curse, and in you all the families of the earth will be blessed.
>
> —Genesis 12:1–3

Imagine how you would feel if God suddenly spoke to you and said, "Pack your things. It's time to move."

If you're anything like me, you'd probably ask, "Move? Can You give me a few more details? Where do You want me to go? And why?"

If the only response was, "Never mind that—I'll tell you when you get there," would you do it? Abraham did. And what makes his decision even more extraordinary is that he was seventy-five years old at the time. He was certainly set in his ways and comfortable with his life. He was no young wanderer looking for adventure. Yet God was calling him to leave behind all he had ever known and start over in a culture that was foreign to him. He had absolutely no idea what awaited him there, but he trusted God and started packing.

If I had been in Abraham's sandals, I probably would have done a lot of complaining and moaning before I finally started packing. I'm just being honest here. I might have done what God asked, but not nearly as quickly as Abraham did.

I know that's true because when I was a young leader at the ripe old age of thirty-three, God called me to leave my comfortable home in Rochester, New York, and move to Russia. There were plenty of reasons I didn't dance for joy when I first sensed God was telling me that I might want to start developing an appetite for borscht. I loved the community I lived in. I loved the new home I had just completely renovated. And more than anything else, I loved the people who made up the congregation where I served as a Messianic rabbi. They were dear, caring people who looked to me for spiritual instruction and guidance. I convinced myself that they needed me. Surely God wouldn't call me away from them. Had I heard Him wrong? It took several months of soul-searching and arguing with God before I told my congregation that I was leaving for Russia, and began making preparations to go.

Life wasn't particularly easy for me in Russia. Winters are bitterly cold. Winter nights in St. Petersburg were long and dark. I didn't know the language. The food took some getting used to, as did the Russian customs. I would be lying if I told you that life in Russia was a picnic. Far from it, in fact. I experienced many trials during my time there, but they were greatly outweighed by the joy I experienced knowing I was living in obedience to God's will and seeing so many lives transformed through the gospel. Because I was obedient to God, He used me to share His love with tens of thousands of people—many of them Jews—who had lived in darkness for decades under Communist rule. (I've already told you about one of my most trying experiences in Russia, when members of my team clashed with Jew-haters there. If you'd like to know more about what happened during my time in Russia, I want to invite you to read my book *A Rabbi Looks at the Last Days*.)

My intention is not to compare myself favorably to Abraham. Rather, I want to illustrate how obedient and courageous Abraham was to obey God. He didn't even know where God was calling him to go when he left—at least I knew that much! The Bible tells us:

> So Abram went, just as *Adonai* had spoken to him. Also Lot went with him. (Now Abram was 75 years old when he departed from Haran.) Abram took Sarai his wife, and Lot his nephew, and all their possessions that they had acquired, and the people that they acquired in Haran, and they left to go to the land of Canaan, and they entered the land of Canaan. Abram passed through the land as far as the place of Shechem, as far as Moreh's big tree. (The Canaanites were in the land then.) Then *Adonai* appeared to Abram, and said, "I will give this land to your seed." So there he built an altar to *Adonai*, who had appeared to him.
>
> —Genesis 12:4–7

I believe one of the most interesting aspects of this story is that God did not decide to bless the patriarch just because of his obedience. Yes, God made demands on Abraham—great demands. But He pronounced the blessing at the same time He told Abraham to pack up and move. Abraham didn't do something that made him especially deserving of God's blessing. He received the blessing because God loved him and chose him—just as He chose you and me. It all comes down to grace and God's sovereignty. God blesses because it is His heart's desire to do so. He blesses the Jewish people because they are Abraham's seed and He always honors His promises.

Note what Paul reveals in Romans 11:28–29:

> Concerning the Good News, they are hostile for your sake; but concerning chosenness, they are loved on account of the fathers—for the gifts and the calling of God are irrevocable.

One of the things I want to mention here is that God gave Abraham and his descendants the right to the land that is today the modern State of Israel. In fact, only a relatively small portion of that land makes up the State of Israel; the original "land grant" decreed to Abraham and his descendants is much larger. This land was given to them by the One who created it, and no one has the right to take it away—or to give it away!

Does God love the Palestinian people? Absolutely. Did He send His Son to die for Arabs all over the world? Of course He did. As the Book of Acts says, "Then Peter opened his mouth and said, 'I truly understand that God is not one to show favoritism, but in every nation the one who fears Him and does what is right is acceptable to Him'" (Acts 10:34–35). God loves the Arab as much as He loves the Jew; He loves the Palestinian and Israeli equally. But this doesn't change the fact that God made a lasting decree to give land in the Middle East that is today Israel to the descendants of Abraham through Isaac and Jacob. There are numerous scriptures that support this:

> After Lot separated himself from him, *ADONAI* had said to Abram, "lift up your eyes, now, and look from the place

> where you are, to the north, south, east and west. For all the land that you are looking at, I will give to you and to your seed forever. I will make your seed like the dust of the earth so that if one could count the dust of the earth, then your seed could also be counted. Get up! Walk about the land through its length and width—for I will give it to you."
>
> —GENESIS 13:14–17

> Remember Abraham, Isaac and Israel, Your servants, to whom You swore by Your own self, and said to them, "I will multiply your seed as the stars of heaven, and all this land that I have spoken of I will give to your offspring, and they will inherit it forever."
>
> —EXODUS 32:13

> Are You not our God who drove out the inhabitants of this land before Your people Israel and gave it to the descendants of Your friend Abraham forever?
>
> —2 CHRONICLES 20:7

The second key to unlocking the prophetic mysteries of Israel is to understand that God has pronounced an eternal blessing upon the children of Israel and He has not rescinded it. Those who bless the Jewish people will be blessed. Those who curse them will be cursed.

In their book *Charting the End Times*, Tim LaHaye and Thomas Ice write: "God's promises to Abraham and Israel are unconditional and guaranteed through the various subsequent covenants. A definite pattern for Israel's future history was prophesied in Deuteronomy before the Jews set even one foot in the Promised Land (Deuteronomy 4:28–31). The predicted pattern for God's program with Israel was to be as follows: They would enter the land under Joshua, and they would eventually turn away from the Lord and be expelled from the land and scattered among the Gentile nations. From there the Lord would regather the Jewish people during the latter days."[1] The Bible is filled with this promise that God will regather the Jewish people in the last days. He is regathering them back to their land physically and to Himself spiritually through His promised Messiah, Yeshua.

Are You on God's Side?

During the Civil War, Abraham Lincoln responded to a man who asked if he believed God was on the Union's side in the conflict. Said Lincoln, "Sir, my greatest concern is not whether God is on our side; my greatest concern is to be on God's side, for God is always right."[2] Anyone on the side fighting against the Jews is on the wrong side. And now more than ever, as we embark on the end of the age, it is important to be on the right side!

I've often quoted Dennis Prager, who wrote, "Look at who most blesses the Jews and who most curses them, and you decide whether the verse in Genesis has validity."[3] Prager goes on to talk about the hatred for the Jews that permeates the Arab world and says, "...that part of the world lags behind the rest of humanity, including in most instances sub-Saharan Africa, in virtually every social, moral and intellectual indicator. And there is no question but that its half-century long preoccupation with destroying Israel has only increased the Arab world's woes."[4]

Genesis 12:3 plainly states that nations that bless Israel will in turn be blessed. And I believe the same is true of individuals. I had a friend who was born into an impoverished community in one of the world's poorest countries, Burkina Faso in West Africa. He was slightly better off than most of his neighbors because his father was a shaman, a witch doctor who performed healings, told fortunes, and cast curses for a fee.

All his life, Ram was being prepared to follow in his father's footsteps. But one day, he wandered into a revival meeting being held by Christian missionaries. There he experienced the power and presence of God. He accepted the Messiah, Yeshua, as his Lord and turned away from his plans to become a shaman.

Somehow he managed to get a Bible in his own language and began reading, starting with the first chapter of Genesis. When he reached the twelfth chapter and read God's blessing to Abraham, he took it to heart. God wanted him to bless Israel, so that's what he determined to do. Somehow he managed to scrape together four dollars, and he sent it to an organization that worked to bless believers in Israel. I say "somehow" because the average daily wage in Burkina Faso at the time was around one dollar, and even less for some people. Four dollars was almost a week's wage.

Every year, Ram would send a special gift to bless Messianic believers in Israel. The second year, he sent six dollars; the third year, eight dollars; and then twelve dollars. Year after year, God blessed, and my friend believed that one of the most important reasons was his faithful support of Israel. In the meantime, he was doing everything he could to tell his friends and neighbors about new life through Yeshua.

A few years back, Ram came to Phoenix and appeared on my television show, *Jewish Voice With Jonathan Bernis*. Shortly before he came to Phoenix, Ram had been in Israel, where he dropped off a gift of twenty-eight thousand dollars to help struggling Jewish families. This represented a tithe from the one hundred churches he has planted throughout Burkina Faso. Those churches now have a combined membership of over one hundred thousand people—this in a country where the majority of the population is Muslim and fewer than 25 percent of the people consider themselves Christians.

That twenty-eight thousand dollars sounds like a great deal of money when you consider that it came from poor people in Africa, most of whom are subsistence farmers. But it becomes enormous when you discover that Ram's church has presented several gifts of that amount to bless Israel this year. Ram's eyes shine with joy when he tells you that he and his congregation have been blessed because they made it a priority to bless Israel. And he is not alone. I have met so many ministry partners of Jewish Voice over the years who have shared amazing stories of how God has blessed them as they have blessed the Jewish people. Yes, the promise stands strong today. Bless Israel and you will be blessed.

Does this mean God expects you to endorse everything Israel does? My answer is the same one Peter gave when he and the other apostles were ordered to stop talking about Yeshua: "We ought to obey God rather than men" (Acts 5:29, KJV). In other words, if the present government of Israel does things that are in direct conflict with the Word of God, then those things should be opposed. The government of Israel is not acting as God's infallible agent. Its leaders can and do make decisions that should be criticized.

But criticism can be delivered in a constructive and helpful way. And anyone who opposes policies of the Israeli government should make sure he or she is doing so for good reasons and not due to any latent anti-Semitic attitudes toward the Jewish people. Not long ago I read about a grocery co-op that was refusing to carry produce from Israel because it was grown on so-called stolen land.[5] There is nothing "stolen" about the land Israel sits on.

I WILL CURSE THOSE WHO CURSE YOU

In fact, every time we pressure Israel to give up some of its land, something terrible seems to happen. My good friend Bill Koenig lays out example after example in his book *Eye to Eye*, which I encourage you to read. Here are a few instances:[6]

- In 1994, when President Bill Clinton met with Syria's President Hafez el-Assad in Geneva, the two talked about getting Israel to relinquish the Golan Heights to Palestinian control. The next day, the Northridge earthquake struck Southern California, killing nearly sixty people, leaving twenty thousand homeless, and causing more than $20 billion in property damage.[7]

- Five years later, on May 3, 1999, backed by the support of the United States government, Yasser Arafat was scheduled to declare the formation of a Palestinian state with Jerusalem as its capital. It never happened because powerful tornadoes swept across Oklahoma and Kansas, causing more than $1 billion worth of damage. President Bill Clinton asked Arafat to postpone his declaration until December.[8]

- In August of 2005, Israeli Prime Minister Ariel Sharon announced the implementation of a "disengagement plan" in which Jewish settlers were to be evicted from the homes they had built in the Gaza Strip. The move was primarily the result of pressure from the United States government. Before it could be put into action, meteorologists reported that a hurricane was forming in the Atlantic. They called it Katrina.[9]

As I said in my book *A Rabbi Looks at the Last Days*, there are far too many incidents to be coincidental:

> I do not think for a moment that God sent these calamities upon the American people. Instead, I believe He lifted His hand of protection, and we were battered by one disaster after another. Only God knows what would befall our nation if He completely lifted His protection from us. Only in the world to come will we know how often He has stretched out His hand to protect us, individually and as a nation.[10]

There are so many instances in which those who raised their hands against Israel have found themselves fighting against God. Consider the Six-Day War of 1967, in which God protected Israel from three of its antagonistic neighbors—Syria, Jordan, and Egypt. As the war drew near, it seemed that Israel was about to be wiped off the map. Israel had around 275,000 troops, compared to 456,000 soldiers from the Arab countries. Israel's enemies also had a clear advantage with regard to weaponry, including twice as many tanks and about four times as many aircraft.[11]

According to the Jewish organization Chabad, "So pessimistic was the outlook that the nation's cemeteries and national parks were marked to become gravesites for the many who would surely perish in the course of the war. However, despite all the prognostications, by the time the war ended, the territory under Israeli control had tripled in size. Jews returned to sites where their ancestors had lived for thousands of years, sites from which waves of terror were launched against them for so many years. The casualties and losses were painful, but minimal in comparison to all projections. The Jewish nation was miraculously victorious in the face of unbelievable odds."[12]

It was Independence Day in Israel when Egyptian artillery and troops began moving into the Sinai Desert. Syria and Jordan put their armed forces on alert and announced they would respond if

Israel "attacked" Egypt. But, of course, Israel could not sit idly by and do nothing while Egyptian troops and tanks moved into position along its borders. It is true that Israel fired the first shot in the war, but it was clear that it was about to be attacked. There is no other reasonable explanation for Egypt's push into the Sinai.

The war was over in six days, with Israel clearly victorious. By the time the fighting stopped, Israel had control of the Gaza Strip, the Sinai Peninsula, the West Bank (which includes Bethlehem and East Jerusalem), and the Golan Heights.

This wasn't the first or last time that Israel was victorious in a war with its Arab neighbors. The first occurred in 1948, shortly after the State of Israel came into being. In that conflict, Israel found herself battling the surrounding nations of Egypt, Jordan, Lebanon, Syria, and Iraq. In the early days of the war, it seemed certain that Arab forces would sweep to victory. Israel was totally unprepared for battle, and the Arab forces were bolstered by hundreds of volunteers from Middle Eastern countries that were not officially involved in the conflict. The invaders inflicted heavy casualties and bombed major highways throughout Israel, thus temporarily blocking the movement of Israeli troops.

In 1948, as in 1967, the Arab forces far outnumbered their Israeli counterparts, and they were much better armed. More than six thousand Israelis lost their lives in the conflict, making it the bloodiest and most costly war in Israel's history. But as God said in Genesis 12:3, "I will bless those who bless you, and whoever curses you I will curse" (NIV).

Just when it seemed that Israel's defeat was sure, the tables turned suddenly and dramatically. Israeli troops began pushing the invaders out of the country and regaining territory that had been lost. By the end of the war, Israel had added five thousand square kilometers of territory.[13]

The Old Testament is full of similar stories from Israel's history. God delivered the Israelites from the hand of the Moabites and Ammonites in the days of King Jehoshaphat in 2 Chronicles chapter 20. And a similar story is found in 2 Kings chapter 19. In this instance, King Sennacherib of Assyria demanded that Israel surrender to him or else be destroyed. He mocked the God of Israel and told King Hezekiah of the many other kingdoms that had fallen to his army. But Hezekiah took the matter to God in prayer and received this reply:

> "He [King Sennacherib] will not come to this city, or shoot an arrow there, or come before it with a shield, or throw up a siege-ramp against it. By the way that he came, by the same he will return, and he will not come into this city"—it is a declaration of *ADONAI*. "For I will defend this city to save it, for My own sake, and for My servant David's sake."
>
> —2 KINGS 19:32–34

The Bible goes on to say, "Then it came about that night that the angel of *ADONAI* went out and struck down 185,000 men in the Assyrian camp. When the men arose early in the morning, behold, they were all dead corpses. So King Sennacherib of Assyria withdrew, went away, and returned home, and stayed in Nineveh. One day, as he was worshipping in the house of his god Nisroch, his sons Adrammelech and Sarezer struck him down with the sword, and escaped to the land of Ararat. Then his son Esarhaddon became king in his place" (2 Kings 19:35–37).

IF WE ARE ON GOD'S SIDE, WE WIN!

If God is for us, it doesn't matter who is against us. If we are standing with Him and blessing His people, we have no reason to fear any wars or battles to come. All of Israel's ancient enemies have disappeared. The Philistines are gone. So are the Amalekites, the Assyrians, and the Babylonians. Most of these cultures disappeared centuries ago. And yet God's chosen people survive—and not only survive, but thrive!

In modern times, I think of the Soviet Union. Although the Soviets never fought an actual war with Israel, many battles were fought with the weapons they provided to its enemies. The Soviets constantly took an anti-Israeli stance in the United Nations and in their international policies. Of course, that's not surprising since the Soviet Union was officially against all religions. But I believe the Soviet Union's dissolution was directly tied to its opposition to and harsh treatment of Israel.

Once again, I sincerely believe that we are in the last days of planet Earth, the time when all of the remaining prophecies of the Bible will be fulfilled. At the same time, I understand that God is not bound by time, and that because He is eternal and exists outside of time, with Him a thousand years is as a single day (Ps. 90:4). I also know that Yeshua said no one knows the day or hour of His return (Matt. 24:36; Mark 13:32). But He also said we would be able to see the signs of His return. I believe those signs are all around us. Now, more than ever, we need to be on His side. And that means, among other things, we must stand with Israel and the Jewish people.

The Jewish people have blessed the world in countless ways. For instance, since the Nobel Prize was first awarded in 1895, some 22 percent of all recipients have been Jewish. In fact, Jewish recipients of the Nobel Prize represent:

- 41 percent of all those awarded in economics;
- 28 percent of those awarded in medicine;

- 26 percent of those awarded in physics;
- 19 percent of those awarded in chemistry;
- 13 percent of those awarded in literature.[14]

In 2013, six of the eight Nobel prizes awarded were to Jews. Yet the Jewish people make up only one-quarter of 1 percent of the world's population.[15] Clearly their contributions in the arts, sciences, medicine, and literature are disproportionate to their size.

We also need to consider the spiritual blessings given to the world through the Jewish people:

- The Messiah Himself was a Jew by birth.
- The Jews preserved the Old Testament Scriptures—and were used by God to write all twenty-seven books of the New Testament (with the possible exception of Luke, who wrote Acts and possibly Hebrews—although most believe the "beloved physician" was indeed of Jewish background).

Paul lists the spiritual blessings given to and through the Jewish people in Romans 9:4–5: "To them belong the adoption and the glory and the covenants and the giving of the *Torah* and the Temple service and the promises. To them belong the patriarchs—and from them, according to the flesh, the Messiah, who is over all, God, blessed forever. Amen."

How Can We Bless the Jewish People?

There are many ways we can obey the Bible's command to bless the Jewish people. First, and most important, we must pray for the

Jewish people to come to know their Messiah. I believe what Yeshua said in John 6:44: "No one can come to Me unless My Father who sent Me draws him—and I will raise him up on the last day." This means prayer is required to draw anyone to faith in Messiah. I became a believer when I was twenty years old in college because a friend came to faith, started praying for me, and then got all her new Christian friends to pray for me by name. I believe it was their prayers that caused me, in just a matter of months, to go to a Bible study with her and invite Yeshua into my life.

Are you praying for your Jewish friends, neighbors, and coworkers? If not, I urge you to start praying for them daily. They are not in your life by accident.

Psalm 122:6 exhorts us to "pray for the peace of Jerusalem." The Hebrew word translated "peace" in this verse is the word *shalom*. The fullest translation of *shalom* is "to bring to completion." In other words, God wants His eternal plan to be fulfilled, to be brought to completion concerning the land and people of Israel. In fact, the only peace plan that can succeed in the Middle East is God's peace plan through the Prince of Peace. World-renowned Bible teacher Derek Prince wrote, "Nations determine their destiny by how they respond to the restoration of God's people."[16] He went on to say:

> Now for the promise—a beautiful and familiar blessing for those who align themselves with God's purposes for Jerusalem, for Israel and for God's people: "Pray for the peace of Jerusalem: they shall prosper that love thee" (Psalm 122:6, KJV).... We have to actively identify ourselves with what God is saying in His Word and what He is doing in history. The primary way we can do so is to identify with what God is doing through our prayers. We can pray for the peace of Jerusalem. For the restoration of Jerusalem. For Jerusalem to become all that God has declared in the

> Scriptures Jerusalem shall be. To those who pray and are concerned, this is the promise: "They shall prosper that love thee."[17]

This is absolutely true for every nation on Earth, including the United States. Nations that stand up for and support Israel are blessed by God. Nations that turn against Israel fall under a curse. They may experience internal strife, rampant crime, poverty, and other evils. Throughout history many nations and peoples who cursed Israel were destroyed for coming against the "apple of His eye" (Zech. 2:12).

America's leaders will be making a grave mistake if they turn against Israel or think we don't need to stand with Israel. We must be very careful in our dealings with the nation of Israel and the Jewish people. Does this mean we support Israel carte blanche in everything they do? Certainly not. But it does mean that in everything we do, even when there may be disagreement, our desire must to be to support and bless Israel, even when we bless through constructive criticism.

Second, we need to proclaim. Romans 1:16 tells us that the gospel is the power of God unto salvation to all who believe, to the Jew first and also to the nations. I believe this is a biblical principle that is still in effect today, not just a statement of history that the gospel message began with the Jewish people. Paul, the apostle to the Gentiles, followed this principle, and in every city to which he traveled, he always went first to the synagogue to share the gospel of the Messiah.

Jewish people do not have a different path to salvation than Gentiles do, as I have heard some wrongly teach. This erroneous doctrine, known as "dual covenant theology," began after the Holocaust in an effort to heal the divide that existed between the church and synagogue. Although well-meaning, it sadly undercuts the truth of the gospel—that all need salvation through Jesus, the Messiah. Jesus Himself declared that He was the Way, the Truth, and the Life, and that no one could come to the Father except through Him (John 14:6). His is the only name "under heaven given to mankind by which we must be saved" (Acts 4:12).

The apostle Paul asks the question: How can they hear unless someone proclaims, and how can they proclaim unless one be sent? For faith comes by hearing and hearing by the Word of God (Rom. 10:14–17). If you look at this passage in context, it is talking about the salvation of Israel. All they need to do to be saved is to believe. And they will believe only after they have heard. So who is going to tell them? I believe this is your job. The church—and, more specifically, you as part of that church—has been called to "provoke Israel to jealousy" (Rom. 11:11). How do you do this? By possessing something they want but do not have.

You have to not only tell them but also show them you have a living, vibrant relationship with their God through their Messiah. You have to demonstrate for them true love, a peace that passes all understanding, a sense of purpose and destiny, and a divine connection to a living God who answers prayer. Now is the time to facilitate Yeshua's return by sharing your faith with the Jewish people the Lord has assigned you to reach. If you don't have any Jewish friends to share with, ask the Lord to bring some Jewish people into your life whom you can impact. Why not come with us on one of our Jewish Voice outreaches to Jewish communities in need in places such as Ethiopia, Zimbabwe, and Ukraine? We have lots of opportunities. All you have to do is be willing and available.

Finally, you can give. There are many ministries like Jewish Voice that have a specific mandate to reach Jewish people with the good news. Do you know how much of your church's missions budget is going to reaching the Jewish people with the gospel? If it is insignificant or nothing at all, will you work to help change this? Remember the story of the Roman centurion's servant whom Jesus healed? Luke 7 records why: "'This man deserves to have you do this, because he loves our nation and has built our synagogue.' So Jesus went with them" (4–6, NIV). Blessing follows those who financially bless Israel, and the greatest blessing you can give them is the gospel.

You can also support organizations that are working to help impoverished Jews in Israel and around the world. There are a number of Messianic Jewish organizations that are helping Jewish families around the world escape from persecution, relocate to Israel, and rebuild their lives there. Many of these organizations are providing essentials such as food, clothing, and shelter for the people of Israel. Did you know that more than one-third of Israel's people live beneath the poverty line and many struggle to survive? Some are elderly widows and widowers who suffered through the terror of the Holocaust. Now in their old age, when they should be comforted and cared for, they find themselves suffering from the terrors of chronic hunger, sickness, and poverty. Your giving can help support those bringing them relief.

STAND UP FOR ISRAEL AND THE JEWISH PEOPLE

I also want to urge you to stand up for the Jewish people. Make up your mind that you will not be silent in the face of anti-Semitism. Urge your government representatives to support Israel. Stand against the BDS (Boycott, Divestment, and Sanctions) movement, which is a sinister effort to damage Israel economically. If you've never heard of this movement, find out more and then speak out. It is rapidly overtaking college campuses and polluting the views of

Christian young people toward Israel. Let your voice be heard. You can make a difference.

The second key to unlocking the prophetic mysteries of Israel is to understand that the principle of divine blessing and cursing based on how nations and individuals treat the Jewish people is still in effect. How we align ourselves with this decree will determine whether God blesses us or not. So be blessed. Be a conduit of blessing to the Jewish people. And the greatest blessing you can give them is the gospel!

Chapter 3

KEY THREE: THE NEW COVENANT

"Behold, days are coming"—it is a declaration of ADONAI—
"when I will make a new covenant with the house
of Israel and with the house of Judah.... I will put My
Torah within them. Yes, I will write it on their heart. I
will be their God and they will be My people."
—JEREMIAH 31:30, 32

THE PROPHET JEREMIAH was born during a very difficult period in Israel's history. The glorious kingdom under David and Solomon had been divided in two—Judah in the south and Israel in the north. The northern kingdom of Israel had been overrun by the Assyrians in 722 BC. Then, a century and a half later, the southern kingdom of Judah was defeated by the Babylonians.

Jerusalem lay in ruins, and the temple was destroyed. Most of the population was in captivity in Babylon.

Jeremiah served as a prophet of God for more than forty years, ministering during the rule of five kings of Judah—Josiah, Jehoahaz, Jehoiakim, Jehoiachin, and Zedekiah. During this time he wrote the Books of Jeremiah and Lamentations, which speak of the sad situation that had befallen the Jewish people because of their disobedience. In Lamentations, Jeremiah writes of children dying in the streets from hunger—of mothers eating their own children in a desperate attempt to fight off starvation.

Consider this passage from the second chapter of Lamentations:

> My eyes are filled with tears. My stomach is in torment. My heart is poured out on the ground over the destruction of the daughter of my people—as young children and infants languish in the city squares. They say to their mothers, "Where is grain and wine?" as they faint like a wounded soldier in the city squares, as their lives ebb away in their mothers' bosom.
>
> —Lamentations 2:11–12

Despite the horrors the Jews of the southern kingdom of Judah were living through, God had neither forsaken nor forgotten them. Suffering would not last forever. God would rescue and redeem His people. It was just as true then as it is today: "Weeping may stay for the night, but joy comes in the morning" (Ps. 30:6).

Speaking through Jeremiah, God declared that a day was coming when the children of Israel would be forgiven and restored as a nation. This is what the passage in Jeremiah 31 is referring to—a new covenant, when God would relate to His people in a new and intimate way. Thus, the third key to unlocking the prophetic mysteries of Israel is to understand the new covenant God promised to and through the Jewish people.

God Won't Desert His People

When the Babylonians defeated the Jews and thousands of them were carried off into captivity, many fell into despair and thought God had given up on them and rejected them for their sin. But this was never the case. He did not say to them, "I provided for you through the wilderness, and yet you've continued to be disobedient. You've continued to be rebellious and you've continued to break My covenant, so I'm done with you. I'm going to turn to a new nation because I just can't take your disobedience anymore. I've reached the end of My rope." No, He did not say anything of the sort.

But this is what the dangerous lie of replacement theology teaches. You may have never heard of replacement theology, but you can trust me when I tell you that this teaching—also known as supersessionism—is running rampant once again in the evangelical Christian church. This errant theology teaches that God reached a point where He was totally fed up with the Jewish people. As a result of this, the covenant relationship He once had with Abraham's physical seed has been annulled and transferred to the church, the new Israel.

Now, while it is true that Gentile believers become Abraham's spiritual heirs through the Messiah, there is no scripture anywhere that suggests God will break His covenant with the Jewish people. Instead, believers who are not from a Jewish background have been grafted into the natural olive tree, Israel, as wild branches. This engrafting includes a warning: "do not boast against the [natural] branches. But if you do boast, it is not you who support the root but the root supports you" (Rom. 11:18).

Far from revoking His covenant with the Jews, God says, "I'm going to give you a new, better covenant with better promises and more power." Here are four important aspects of this new covenant that are important to understand.

1. It is internal rather than external.

God is going to write this covenant on the hearts of His people. Some Bible translations say it will be written on the "hearts and minds" of His people. (For instance, see Jeremiah 31:33 in the NET Bible.) This is in direct contrast to the Mosaic Law, which was written on tablets of stone and later parchment. The Mosaic covenant rests on our shoulders like a heavy mantle, with assorted rules and laws we can never fully keep. Although we may attempt to do so with great diligence, it is simply impossible.

In the Book of Galatians, Paul says we are no longer under the law. Some teachers claim this means the law has disappeared and no longer exists, but that is inaccurate. Rather, the law has been taken off tablets of stone and parchment, and inscribed on our hearts. And because of this, we have been given the power to be "doers of the word" (James 1:22) through the indwelling of the Holy Spirit.

Let me give a quick illustration from my own experience. I grew up with the Ten Commandments. I had known them since my early childhood. One of these commandments is "Thou shalt not steal" (Exod. 20:15, KJV). Still, I stole. And I justified this behavior. "After all," I thought, "I am a poor college student. The store makes a profit on me. So if I buy the cheap canned goods and slide a can of expensive macadamia nuts into the pocket of my army jacket, I'm really not stealing. I'm just lowering the store's profit margin slightly." That was my perspective until I became a believer in Yeshua. This time, after I walked out of the store with the stolen macadamia nuts in my pocket, I heard a voice inside me softly say, "Thou shalt not steal." This was a new experience for me. I was so convicted, I eventually walked back into the store and slipped the can of macadamia nuts back onto the shelf where I found them.

What happened to me? The commandment to not steal was external to me under the law. But when I came to know Yeshua, it was internalized. It was written on my heart through the new covenant and became personal to me.

2. The new covenant is about a relationship.

The second element of the new covenant is revealed when God says, "I will be their God and they will be My people" (Jer. 31:32). The new covenant is about a relationship between God the Creator and His people. It involves knowing God instead of knowing about Him.

This is very different from the relationship that existed between God and His people during the Mosaic covenant. Under that covenant, the people were able to see the glory of God in the tabernacle and the temple, but they couldn't touch the presence of God. If they touched the ark of the covenant or dared to set their feet on the holy mountain, they would be killed. We are protected from death under the new covenant because we have the status of God's sons and daughters.

While it is true that we are all God's creation, we are not all His children until we cry out to Him and are born from above. (See John 3:5.) As the Gospel of John reveals, "But whoever did receive Him, those trusting in His name, to these He gave the right to become children of God" (John 1:12). This relationship is an adoptive, personal relationship with the living God. Under the new covenant, He is no longer just our Lord; He is now also *Abba* (Daddy). Through our faith, He has given us the authority to become His children. This is the unique relationship the new covenant provides for us.

In the Book of Romans, Paul elaborates on this new covenant we have entered into through the atoning work of the Messiah:

> For you did not receive the spirit of slavery to fall again into fear; rather, you received the Spirit of adoption, by whom we cry, "*Abba*! Father!" The *Ruach* Himself bears witness with our spirit that we are children of God. And if children, also heirs—heirs of God and joint-heirs with Messiah—if indeed we suffer with Him so that we may also be glorified with Him.
>
> —Romans 8:15–17

We now have an intimacy with God that allows us to access the holy of holies, so we can go boldly before God's throne any time we desire. How would you feel if you had a personal audience with the president of the United States? Would you feel nervous? Would you take some time to rehearse what you were going to say? You'd probably spend a lot of time deciding what to wear and looking in the mirror to make sure everything was perfect.

Most of us are at least a little bit in awe of authority and celebrity. But there is no greater luminary than God, and most of us come into His presence without giving it a second thought. And that's OK because that's the way He wants it. If you need Him in the middle of the night, He's there. If you're sitting in your car in the middle of a traffic jam, He's available to talk to you then. He doesn't care if your hair is neatly combed, if you've done your makeup, or if you're wearing a jacket and tie. He's never too busy or preoccupied to talk to you. After all, you are His child!

This is the type of relationship available to us through the new covenant. It is a promise made first to Israel—the Jewish people, the children of Abraham. The promise is that there will be a time of adoption, a relationship with God unlike what they've known under the Mosaic law. That time is here. And it is a promise you have inherited though the Messiah of Israel, Yeshua.

3. All Israel shall be saved.

The third element of the new covenant is that the day will come when all Israel will be saved:

> No longer will each teach his neighbor or each his brother, saying: "Know *Adonai*," for they will all know Me, from the least of them to the greatest.
>
> —Jeremiah 31:33

This promise is yet to be fulfilled, but it will come to pass—and I believe it will happen soon. This verse refers to a time in history when either all or the vast majority of the Jewish people will know their God intimately.

In Romans 11:25–27 (nkjv), Paul expounds on this promise from Jeremiah 31 when he writes:

> For I do not desire, brethren, that you should be ignorant of this mystery, lest you should be wise in your own opinion, that blindness in part has happened to Israel until the fullness of the Gentiles has come in. And so all Israel will be saved, as it is written: "The Deliverer will come out of Zion, and He will turn away ungodliness from Jacob; for this is My covenant with them, when I take away their sins."

This is one of the most important teachings in the New Testament concerning the Jewish people. It may, in fact, be the most important. We learn from these verses that:

The Jewish people are experiencing a spiritual blindness.

This blindness is keeping them from recognizing Jesus as their promised Messiah. Contrary to what many Christians understand, this does not mean that God struck the Jews with blindness because they failed to accept Jesus as their Messiah. Rather, it means that many Jews failed to accept Him because they were already blind and thus didn't recognize Him for who He is. This is good news for non-Jews because it was through the Jews' blindness that the door to salvation was opened to the Gentiles.

This blindness is partial.

We are also told this blindness—or, as some translations say, this hardening—is *in part*, or *partial*. This does not mean they have poor eyesight, like a near-blind individual who needs to wear thick, Coke-bottle glasses to see. Rather, it means Israel is divided into two groups—those who are blinded and those who can see. In other words, not all Jewish people are blinded to their Messiah. There is (and always has been) a remnant of Jews who do recognize Jesus as Yeshua, Israel's Messiah and the Savior of all mankind. Many of these Jewish believers in Jesus identify as Messianic Jews, meaning they are Jews who have accepted their Messiah but have not left their Jewish heritage and identity.

Many Jewish people have told me that they would never be able to accept Yeshua as the Messiah because we Jewish people "settled the issue" in the first century. Our rabbis rejected Him and that's all there was to it.

But that's not completely accurate. In the two thousand years since Yeshua walked the streets of Jerusalem, there has never been a time when there were no Jewish believers. Jews who have openly expressed their faith in the man from Nazareth include Abd-al-Masih, who was martyred for his faith; Michael Solomon Alexander, a former rabbi who became the first Anglican Bishop of Jerusalem; Jean-Marie Lustiger, who went on to be the Roman Catholic Archbishop of Paris; and Israel Zolli, who served as Chief Rabbi of Rome before turning his life over to Yeshua![1]

As my friend Dr. Michael L. Brown writes, "Jews have always believed in Jesus. In fact, in the beginning, it was *only* Jews who believed in him, and today, there are probably more Jewish believers in Jesus than ever before.... In every generation there has been a faithful remnant of Jews who have followed Jesus the Messiah, numbering from the thousands into the tens of thousands, and they have maintained their faith in spite of often difficult consequences. Right now, there are as many as 150,000 to 200,000 Jewish believers in Jesus worldwide (this is probably a conservative estimate), including American Jews, Russian Jews, South American Jews, and Israeli Jews. Many of them are highly educated, and some are ordained rabbis. Jews *do* believe in Jesus, and their numbers are growing by leaps and bounds."[2]

So again, there have always been Jewish believers, and many of them have paid a great price for their faith—some even losing their lives because of their acceptance of Yeshua. As I wrote in my book *A Rabbi Looks at Jesus of Nazareth*, "Many Gentiles don't seem to understand that it is often a very difficult decision for a Jew to accept Jesus as their Messiah. It is not a matter of praying the sinner's prayer and then going on with your life. It can mean that you are disowned by your family and rejected by life-long friends. The Jewish believer will be made to feel that he or she is 'joining the enemy,' due to the long history of 'the church's' persecution against the Jews."[3]

Michael Brown notes, "Once a learned Jew does believe in Yeshua, he is discredited and so his name is virtually removed from the rolls of history. It's almost as if such people ceased to exist.... The story of Max Wertheimer provides one case in point. In the last century, Wertheimer came to the States as an Orthodox Jew, but over the course of time, he became a Reform Jew and was ordained a rabbi upon graduating from Hebrew Union College in Cincinnati in 1889.

(He also received a PhD from the University of Cincinnati the same year.) He then served as the greatly loved rabbi of B'Nai Yeshurun Synagogue in Dayton, Ohio, for the next ten years. When he became a fervent believer in Jesus, however, pastoring a church as well, his name was literally removed from the rolls of the school—a school of alleged tolerance at that. Why was his name dropped? According to Alfred A. Isaacs, cited in the November 25, 1955, edition of the *National Jewish Post*, Wertheimer was disowned by Hebrew Union College solely because of his Christian faith. And to think, this happened in a 'liberal' Reform Jewish institution!"[4] And yet despite the difficulties, Jews are turning to Yeshua in record numbers.

Please understand, I am not saying you can judge the validity of a movement by the number of those involved. There are more than a billion Muslims in the world today, and I'm convinced they are way off base in what they believe. So are Jehovah's Witnesses, for that matter. We simply can't judge the validity of a movement by counting its adherents. At one time there weren't more than a handful of people who believed in Yeshua, but the powerful truth they upheld changed the world.

Scholar Arnold Fruchtenbaum says: "What is happening now...is what has always happened throughout Jewish history, that is only a remnant believes. It is always the remnant that believes. This was true in Elijah's day and it is true today. The fact that the majority does not believe is not evidence enough that the whole nation has been cut off. The point is that in Israel, past, present, and future, it is the remnant that is faithful to the revelation of Grace....The remnant is always in the nation, not outside of it; the Hebrew Christians, the present-day remnant, are part of Israel and the Jewish people. Their Jewishness is distinct."[5]

This blindness is temporary.

We are told that this blindness or hardening has happened *until*. The day will come when this blindness will be removed and all or a vast majority of the Jewish people will see Yeshua for who He is. Zechariah 12:10 prophesies this day: "Then I will pour out on the house of David and the inhabitants of Jerusalem a spirit of grace and supplication, when they will look toward Me whom they pierced. They will mourn for him as one mourns for an only son and grieve bitterly for him, as one grieves for a firstborn."

It's tragic that most Jewish people have lived with this blindness to their Messiah for the past nineteen hundred years. But remember that a thousand years is only a day to the Lord. And if that is true, nineteen hundred years is less than two days in His sight. What is two days in comparison to an eternity spent seeing our Messiah face-to-face?

This blindness will come off their eyes at a set time in history.

Not only is the blindness of Israel temporary; we are told the specific time when this blindness will be removed, a time Paul calls "the fullness of the Gentiles" (Rom. 11:25). Most end-times teachers interpret this as the "full number of Gentiles." In other words, the blindness will come off the eyes of the Jewish people when the last Gentile is saved, or when the Gentile quota is met.

I do not see it this way. The Greek word *plērōma* (πλήρωμα) can be translated to mean "fullness, filling, fulfillment, or completion."[6] I think what Paul is telling us is there will be an allotted time for the gospel to spread throughout the nations of the world, and when this season is completed, the gospel will once again return to the Jewish people, as Psalm 102:13 declares: "You will arise and have compassion on Zion, for it is time to show favor to her; the appointed time has come" (NIV).

There is much more I could say about this, but I will talk more about the fullness of the Gentiles in chapter 7.

The church must come out of her blindness.

Before we move on from this topic, I want to point out that there is also a blindness that afflicts the church. Many Christians are blind to the Jewish roots of their Christian faith. They have forgotten that it was Israel who gave the world the Messiah, who preserved the Scriptures, who taught us that there is one true God, the Maker of heaven and earth. As the church is delivered from this blindness and begins fulfilling her call to be a light and blessing to Israel, it will pave the way for Israel's restoration to their God and Messiah's return.

The Messiah will return when the blindness comes off the eyes of the Jewish people and embrace Yeshua as their Messiah. This is precisely what Jesus Himself declared over Jerusalem as He wept over the city before His death: "For I tell you, you will never see Me again until you say, '*Baruch ha-ba b'shem* ADONAI. Blessed is He who comes in the name of the LORD!'"(Matt. 23:39).

As authors Tim LaHaye and Thomas Ice write, "Israel's regathering and the turmoil are specific signs that God's end-time program is on the verge of springing into full gear. In addition, the fact that all three streams of prophecy (the nations, Israel, and the church) are converging for the first time in history constitutes a sign in itself. This is why many students of prophecy believe we are near the last days. If you want to know where history is headed, simply keep your eye on what God is doing with Israel."[7]

4. The new covenant is about the forgiveness of sin.

The final aspect of the new covenant that is important to understand is that God will forgive the sins of those who come into this covenant with Him. And not only will He forgive them, but He will also forget those sins completely, as Jeremiah 31:33 says: "For I will forgive their iniquity, their sin I will remember no more."

This forgiveness of sin is in contrast to the Mosaic covenant, with its system of animal sacrifices to cover sin—not remove it, but merely cover it up—so God could dwell in the midst of His people for another year. It is only the blood of Yeshua that is able to wash our sin away and make us absolutely clean so that we become a "new creation" in Messiah (2 Cor. 5:17).

An old Jewish parable tells of a king who got into a heated argument with his son. Enraged by his son's behavior, the king threw the young man out of the kingdom and told him to never return. Years went by and the two men never spoke. The son traveled all over the world but never again set foot in his father's kingdom.

The king often thought of his son and regretted the gulf that had grown up between them. Finally, his longing to see his son grew so great that he sent his top ministers to find the young man and ask him to return home. It took months, but they finally found the young man and told him that his father wanted him to come home, that he was anxious to be reconciled.

The prince shook his head and said he couldn't come home. He had been too hurt by what his father had done, and he felt he would never be able to get over it. With heavy hearts, the ministers traveled back to the king and gave him the bad news. A shadow fell over the king's face when he heard what his son had said. Then his eyes lit up as he realized what to do.

"Go back to my son," he said, "and tell him to come as far as he can. I'll come the rest of the way to meet him."

That is exactly what God does for us. All He requires of us is to take one step in His direction. He'll cover the rest of the distance, even though it may be a billion miles or more. All we have to do is come as far as we can, and He'll come the rest of the way to meet us.

Yeshua told a similar story when He related the parable of the prodigal son. The primary difference was that the father in this parable didn't do anything wrong. The son wound up in a bad place solely because of his own bad behavior. After wasting his inheritance and disgracing his family name, the young man decides to go home and ask his father to take him in as one of the servants. The Bible doesn't even tell us that he was truly sorry for what he had done. His desire to return home was borne out of desperation.

He was hungry and ragged and had no shelter to protect him from the elements. It might even be said that he faced the choice of "go home and apologize to Dad or face a slow, agonizing death." Nevertheless, the Bible says that as soon as that emaciated figure came into view over the horizon—shuffling along as if it was an effort to lift his feet, his shoulders slumped in humiliation and sorrow—"his father saw him and felt compassion. He ran and fell on his neck and kissed him. Then the son said to him, 'Father, I have sinned against heaven and in your presence. I am no longer worthy to be called your son.'

"But the father said to his slaves, 'Quick! Bring out the best robe and put it on him! Put a ring on his hand and sandals on his feet. Bring the fattened calf and kill it! Let's celebrate with a feast! For this son of mine was dead and has come back to life—he was lost and is found!' Then they began to celebrate" (Luke 15:20–24).

There is much more to the story, but I don't want to get sidetracked talking about the elder brother's anger and jealousy. (If you've never read this amazing parable for yourself, I urge you to do it soon.) My point is that the father loved his son so much that he was immediately ready to forgive him. He even ran to meet the boy, something that was considered completely beneath the dignity of a man of his stature—a man who had land and cattle and hired servants. When he saw that his son was coming home, he gladly made a fool of himself. He didn't care what other people thought. His boy was home and that was all that mattered.

As I read Yeshua's parable, I get the feeling that this loving father spent some time every day scanning the dusty horizon, looking for his son—hoping and praying that today would be the day of his return. How many times was he disappointed when what he saw in the distance turned out to be nothing more than dust kicked up by a whirlwind, a wild animal, or a tumbleweed rolling past?

This is a beautiful picture of a spiritual truth. I realize the prodigal son applies to all who have wandered from God, but I also believe Yeshua is referring specifically to Israel in this parable. God is constantly looking for His beloved covenant people who have strayed from Him, hoping that today will be the day of their return. He longs for them to return to Him. They remain the apple of His eye. This is expressed nowhere more beautifully than Isaiah 49:14–15 (NIV):

> But Zion said, "The LORD has forsaken me, the Lord has forgotten me.
>
> "Can a mother forget the baby at her breast and have no compassion on the child she has borne? Though she may forget, I will not forget you!"

Forgiveness is perhaps the single greatest theme of this promised new covenant. The words of Yeshua hanging on the cross ring in my ears as I write. "Father, forgive them; for they know not what they do" (Luke 23:34, KJV). I think forgiveness is one of the greatest themes of the end times. As wickedness grows, so will God's forgiveness and mercy. We will see many come into God's kingdom whom we would never expect to see there.

WHAT? FORGIVE ISIS?

Forgiveness isn't just something God does; it is required of us as well. And believe me, I know it's not always easy. I must confess that whenever I hear about some terrible thing Islamic State terrorists have done, a red hot anger rises up in me. It baffles me that they can be so evil. When I think of all the pain they inflict on innocent children and families through their savagery, I want to see them destroyed forever.

For a moment, I think that if God chose to scoop them all up and drop them into hell, that would be just fine with me. But then I hear the Spirit whispering to me, "Are you praying for them?"

"Praying for ISIS? Of course not."

"But I told you to pray for your enemies."

"Oh, yes. I suppose You did."

It's not easy for me to pray for ISIS terrorists. I still want to see the Islamic State and all other terrorist organizations destroyed—but not the people who belong to them. And so I pray that those individuals will have a revelation of the Messiah and be transformed, just as the apostle Paul was on the road to Damascus (Acts 9:1–31). Even though in the natural I sometimes feel as if I would like to see the terrorist soldiers destroyed by fire and brimstone from above, God's mercy calls me to pray that they would come to know Him and realize they have been deceived by Satan.

Let me assure you again that I hate everything these terrorists do. Their actions are detestable. But I believe that in these last days we will see an outpouring of God's grace that will astound us. Time is growing short, and God wants to save as many as possible.

Why am I making such a big deal about forgiveness? First of all, because it's important to God. Second, because God's people are divided over a myriad of mundane issues that ought not to divide us at all—and sadly, one of the most significant issues dividing the church today is Israel. It used to be Charismatic versus non-Charismatic or those who believed one could lose his salvation versus those who believe in eternal security. Today, the big dividing line seems to be Israel. Why? I believe it is because as we near the end, Israel and the salvation of the Jewish people is becoming a bigger issue to Satan. This is all about spiritual warfare.

Understanding God's new covenant with His chosen people and His commitment to fulfill this covenant is a highly important key to understanding God's end-time plan. And that plan involves you. Yes, you heard me correctly. You have a part to play because in these last days we can expect to see the blindness coming off of the eyes of the Jewish people in greater and greater numbers.

Let me close this chapter by telling you about a woman named Sharon Allen. Sharon was born in Beth Israel Hospital in New York City. Her Hebrew name is Sura Rifka, and she was raised in an observant Jewish home. "From the moment my mom lit the *Shabbos* (Sabbath) candles on Friday evening until one hour after sundown on Saturday night," she notes, "there were certain rules and regulations that we followed." She adds, "They did not make us feel constricted or oppressed. It was our way of showing our love, our respect, and our devotion to God."[8]

Sharon married a Jewish man with a similar family background. Together they had a daughter, Elisa, whose Hebrew name is Chava Leah. However, when Elisa was only a few years old, Sharon and her husband received a Jewish divorce, known as a "Get."

Sharon moved with her daughter to Los Angeles, where she got her real estate license and went to work at an agency owned by a man named Ron Allen. They began dating and were eventually married.

Sharon remembers thinking that there was no such thing as a Jew who believed in Jesus. She and Ron discussed his converting to Judaism, and a few years after their marriage, the discussions grew serious. She told Ron about all the ceremonies that would be required of him for an Orthodox conversion, including the last ceremony in which the convert must renounce his prior beliefs before a Beit Din (rabbinical court). Sharon recalls: "Ron agreed to all of the ceremonies but the last one. He said he just didn't think he could renounce Jesus. *I was horrified!* My husband had never mentioned Jesus, hadn't been to church for more than 30 years, and had never used the words 'Christian,' 'Christ,' or 'New Testament.'"[9]

She was upset and told him she was astonished he could believe in something "so pagan." She decided she would read the Bible so she could prove to him that Jesus was not the Messiah. She began her quest with a very specific prayer. "I prayed to the God of Abraham, Isaac, and Jacob to show me the truth and to help my husband become a Jew."[10]

She began reading, and everywhere she looked she saw Yeshua's footprints. "Within the pages of my Jewish Bible, there is much written concerning the Messiah—where He would be born, how He would live His life, the miracles He would do. The Bible also speaks of His suffering and death. It frightened me because what I read sounded very much like what I heard said about Jesus.... So I bought the Rashi commentaries, the Soncino commentaries....I also brought home texts from the *Babylonian Talmud*, the *Encylopædia Judaica*, *Midrash Rabbah*, *Mishneh Torah* by Maimonides, *Targum Onkelos*....On and on I studied, day after day."[11]

One night proved to be a turning point for her. She was at a meeting at synagogue, and after her rabbi had finished his talk, he called for questions. Sharon raised her hand and asked, "Rabbi, what do you tell someone like me who knows Yiddishkeit, follows Judaism, has a Jewish home, and yet, when I read the Jewish Bible, I see *That Man!!?*"[12]

She could not even bring herself to say the name "Jesus" or "Yeshua." Not after nearly two thousand years of persecution in the name of Jesus Christ and Christianity, she recalls. They just called him "That Man"!

Sharon and her rabbi discussed the Yiddishkeit, Jewish customs, the Bible, and other subjects until midnight. Then the rabbi finally closed the meeting with angry words meant to show Sharon and the others in the room why Jesus could not be the promised Messiah. He shouted that Jesus had committed blasphemy on the cross, and mockingly quoted Him, saying, "My God, my God! Why hast Thou forsaken me?"[13]

Sharon was amazed. In his anger, the rabbi "apparently forgot that the statement Jesus made...was first said by our own beloved King David in Psalm 22. *And would any Jew dare to say that David committed blasphemy?!*"[14]

"That night," Sharon says, "I told my husband and daughter, 'I have no more doubts...Jesus is my Jewish Messiah.'"[15]

Sharon now knows there are Jews who believe in Jesus. She is one. She saw in her own Jewish Bible accompanied by extensive research that the prophesied Messiah of the Jewish Bible is fulfilled in the New Testament Jesus, Yeshua HaMashiach.

She is experiencing the glorious new covenant, and the promise of Scripture is that she will not be alone. As the end draws near, more and more of the Jewish people will discover, as Sharon did, that Jesus is the Jewish Messiah.

Chapter 4

KEY FOUR: THE RESTORATION OF JERUSALEM

Jerusalem will be trampled by the Gentiles until
the times of the Gentiles are fulfilled.
—Luke 21:24

Jerusalem is a city that is dear to my heart. It is where Yeshua taught the multitudes, where He was sacrificed on the cross (as had been prophesied), and where after three days He rose from the dead in fulfillment of Bible prophecy. Great men and women of the Bible have dwelled and worshipped there. Kings David and Solomon bestowed their wisdom and laws from within this historic city's walls, and great prophets went there to worship in the temple.

But perhaps most importantly, Jerusalem is where the Messiah will return to rule and reign during the Messianic age.

It may be difficult for the secular or nonreligious person to understand why this city has played, and continues to play, such an important role in world history. After all, Jerusalem is all of 48.3 square miles and of little significance compared to other commercial and industrial cities. How has 48.3 square miles of earth remained so important in the hearts and minds of so many millions for thousands of years? The answer is that Jerusalem is important because it is important to God.

The story of Jerusalem is not just about brick and mortar that has been conquered, destroyed, and restored. It's a story about a people, a chosen people, tied to a chosen land with a chosen capital. It is eternal. Jerusalem does not just exist in time and space; it is also a spiritual reality. And we are told in Scripture that one day a new Jerusalem will come down from heaven adorned as a bride for her husband (Rev. 21:2). Jerusalem is the nexus in the interaction between God and man, and it is instrumental in the fulfillment of His divine plan. It is intricately intertwined with both the history and destiny of the people of Israel. As such, it is also the focus of Satan's attack against God and his envy and hatred for God's chosen people.

In AD 70, Jerusalem, the city where God's holy temple had stood for hundreds of years, was destroyed and burned by Roman soldiers. The Jewish historian Josephus gives us a harrowing eyewitness account of that terrible day—a day Yeshua foretold in Luke 21 and Matthew 24. Josephus writes:

> These Romans put the Jews to flight, and proceeded as far as the holy house itself. At which time one of the soldiers, without staying for any orders, and without any concern or dread upon him at so great an undertaking, and being

> hurried on by a certain divine fury, snatched somewhat out of the materials that were on fire, and being lifted up by another soldier, he set fire to a golden window, through which there was a passage to the rooms that were round about the holy house, on the north side of it. As the flames went upward, the Jews made a great clamor, such as so mighty an affliction required, and ran together to prevent it; and now they spared not their lives any longer, nor suffered any thing to restrain their force, since that holy house was perishing.... And thus was the holy house burnt down.[1]

In Luke 21:24, Yeshua prophesied that Jerusalem would be trampled by the Gentiles until the times of the Gentiles were fulfilled. Indeed, from the time Jerusalem was destroyed in AD 70 until 1967, Jerusalem was trodden down by nation after conquering nation:

- 70–324 occupied by the Romans
- 324–638 controlled by the Byzantines
- 638–1099 controlled by the Muslims
- 1099–1187 controlled by the Crusaders
- 1187–1259 controlled by the Ayyubid Muslims
- 1259–1516 controlled by the Muslims under the Mamluks
- 1516–1917 occupied by the Ottoman Turks
- 1917–1948 controlled by the British
- 1948–1967 the city is divided as Israel and Jordan vie for control[2]

Then in 1967, as a result of Israel's miraculous victory in the Six-Day War, Jerusalem came back under the control of the Jewish people after almost two thousand years. The fourth key to understanding Israel's role in God's end-time plan is to recognize that there is a coming restoration of Jerusalem, God's eternal capital city and the prophesied location of the Messiah's return.

Before we talk more about what is going on in Jerusalem today, I want to look back at some of the city's history and its spiritual significance.

The Anti-Jerusalem

It is said that you can tell a lot about people from the company they keep. Our friends reveal qualities that we admire and often reflect the type of person we are or would like to be.

Our enemies, on the other hand, stand in stark contrast to us. They hate what we are, what we strive to be, and often what we believe in. In some ways they reveal an even clearer picture of us than our friends. As Franklin Roosevelt said, "I ask you to judge me by the enemies I have made."[3]

Your enemy might be considered an "anti-you." For example, we might say that Satan is, in some ways, the antithesis of Yeshua. Yeshua is holiness and love whereas Satan is evil and hatred. (I am not saying that Satan and Yeshua are equals. Yeshua is God Incarnate, and Satan is a created being.) The city of Jerusalem also has its evil counterpart. This anti-Jerusalem is Babel or Babylon. And we can learn a lot about Jerusalem from Babylon's story.

Back in chapter 1, we talked about how Satan brought sin into the world in the Garden of Eden, bringing God's judgment upon the first human beings and upon himself. Satan did not forget God's promise that the seed of the woman would crush him under His foot. He wasted no time in creating his own city of people who would join him in his battle against God.

Satan's first attempt at creating his own city or anti-Jerusalem appears in the Book of Genesis:

> Then they said, "Come! Let's build ourselves a city, with a tower whose top reaches into heaven. So let's make a name for ourselves, or else we will be scattered over the face of the whole land."
>
> —Genesis 11:4

God took notice of their plan and knew they would succeed if they kept going. So He confused their language and scattered them throughout the land. This effectively ended the construction of this city, which came to be known as Babel, because it is where God confused the languages (Gen. 11:5–9).

What can we learn from this? Well, we know that a city is a place where people come together for work, safety, and friendship, and to seek cooperation to accomplish a purpose that cannot be completed on one's own. To be separated and scattered abroad is to live a life of insecurity, isolation, and unfulfillment.

But to aspire to build a tower with its top in the heavens? This is man attempting to reach heaven on his own terms, apart from God. In fact, an early Midrash version of Genesis reads: "He—God—has no right to choose the upper world for Himself, and to leave the lower world to us; therefore we will build us a tower, with an idol on the top holding a sword, so that it may appear as if it intended to war with God."[4]

In Genesis 11:4, the people of Babel said, "So let's make a name for ourselves." This is a very interesting passage because, as we know, the seed promised by God would come through Noah's son Shem (שֵׁם), which means "name" in Hebrew.[5] The people of Babel may or may not have known of Shem or his descendants, but there can be no doubt that the serpent did. By seeking to "make a name" for themselves, they were declaring their autonomy from God and attempting to set up a lineage in opposition to the promised people who carried the "seed" of salvation. Into whose image would they be conformed? The serpent's, of course. God, knowing all things, recognized that Satan was behind the Babel plan and that his ultimate objective was the destruction of humankind.

Although the tower of Babel was destroyed, the city remained, eventually becoming Babylon, the infamous city whose people in 586 BC destroyed Jerusalem and Solomon's temple. This is by no means a coincidence. Satan has no intention of giving up easily.

THE CITY OF MAN VERSUS THE CITY OF GOD

Let there be no doubt: there is a battle raging in heaven and on Earth, and it has been going on for millennia—in fact, since the day the serpent tempted Eve to eat of the fruit of the tree of the knowledge of good and evil. This is a battle between Satan and God and between the City of Man (the anti-Jerusalem) and the City of God (Jerusalem).

Saint Augustine discussed these two visions of Jerusalem in *City of God*, saying:

> Accordingly, two cities have been formed by two loves: the earthly by the love of self, even to the contempt of God; the heavenly by the love of God, even to the contempt of self. The former, in a word, glories in itself, the latter in the Lord. For the one seeks glory from men; but the greatest glory of the other is God, the witness of conscience. The one lifts up its head in its own glory; the other says to its God, "Thou art my glory, and the lifter up of mine head." In the one, the princes and the nations it subdues are ruled by the love of ruling; in the other, the princes and the subjects serve

> one another in love, the latter obeying, while the former take thought for all. The one delights in its own strength, represented in the persons of its rulers; the other says to its God, "I will love Thee, O Lord, my strength."[6]

The City of Man (the anti-Jerusalem) is always at war with the City of God (Jerusalem), whether that city's name is Babel, Babylon, Rome, Constantinople, Tehran, or Moscow. And it will continue to be at war as long as the serpent can turn the hearts of men against God's love.

Abraham and Jerusalem

We should not fear, however, because God is faithful and His promise of redemption finds an able carrier in the patriarch Abraham.

Abraham, once known as Abram, was not a young man when God commanded him to leave his home and go to the land that would be shown to him. Yet despite this, he did as the Lord commanded. The Book of Hebrews says:

> By faith Abraham obeyed when he was called to go out to a place he was to receive as an inheritance. He went out, not knowing where he was going. By faith he migrated to the land of promise as if it were foreign, dwelling in tents with Isaac and Jacob—fellow heirs of the same promise. For he was waiting for the city that has foundations, whose architect and builder is God.
>
> —Hebrews 11:8–10

On his journey, Abram met Melchizedek, the king of Salem (Jerusalem) and priest of God Most High. During that meeting, Melchizedek offered Abram bread and wine and blessed him, saying, "'Blessed be Abram by *El Elyon*, Creator of heaven and earth, and blessed be *El Elyon*, who gave over your enemies into your hand.' Then Abram gave him a tenth of everything" (Gen. 14:19–20).

Melchizedek is considered a "type" or foreshadowing of Jesus. The seventh chapter of Hebrews talks a great deal about this, drawing from prophetic scriptures in the Old Testament:

- "You are a *Kohen* [priest] forever according to the order of Melchizedek" (Ps. 110:4).
- "Without father, without mother, without genealogy, having neither beginning of days nor end of life but made like *Ben-Elohim* [the Son of God], he remains a *kohen* [priest] for all time" (Heb. 7:3).
- "For such a *Kohen Gadol* [high priest] was fitting for us: holy, guiltless, undefiled, separated from sinners, and exalted above the heavens. He has no need to offer up sacrifices day by day like those other *kohanim g'dolim* [high priests]—first for their own sins and then for the sins of the people. For when He offered up Himself, He did this once for all. For the *Torah* appoints as *kohanim g'dolim* men who have weakness; but the word of the oath, which came after the *Torah*, appoints a Son—made perfect forever" (Heb. 7:26–28).

The Book of Hebrews continues to make connections between Yeshua and the Melchizedekian priesthood. And obviously, the bread and wine Melchizedek offered Abram is symbolic of the bread and wine Yeshua offered His disciples at their last Passover together, which is His body and blood offered in atonement for our sins.

Finally, Abram arrived in the land God had promised him. He

entered the city of Salem, which later became known as Jerusalem. And then Adonai took Abram outside and said:

> "Look up now, at the sky, and count the stars—if you are able to count them." Then He said to him, "So shall your seed be." Then he believed in *ADONAI* and He reckoned it to him as righteousness.
>
> —GENESIS 15:4–6

That was when Abram received a new name from God: Abraham, which means "father of many nations." The Bible tells us that all who have faith in God are counted among Abraham's descendants. Galatians 3:6–9 says:

> Just as Abraham "believed God, and it was credited to him as righteousness," know then that those who have faith are children of Abraham. The Scriptures, foreseeing that God would justify the Gentiles by faith, proclaimed the Good News to Abraham in advance, saying, "All the nations shall be blessed through you." So then, the faithful are blessed along with Abraham, the faithful one.

This is important because it links Gentile Christians with the Jewish people. This gives us a common heritage and makes all of us, like Abraham, fellow sojourners seeking that "city that has foundations, whose architect and builder is God" (Heb. 11:10). Thus Jerusalem, whether it is the temporal, heavenly, or new Jerusalem, is the eternal destination that we, Jew and Christian alike, seek.

FROM DAVID TO THE ROMAN OCCUPATION

Jerusalem has risen, fallen, and risen again numerous times throughout the history of the Jewish people. These cycles correspond to the people's obedience and disobedience to God's laws and His divine plan. Furthermore, we see different kingdoms (or anti-Jerusalems) arise that are Satan's direct attempt to thwart the birth of Messiah, the long-awaited One who will defeat Satan and break the curse that has humankind in its grip.

In the following timeline I have summarized some, though not all, of the major events in this cycle:

- 1000 BC: King David conquers the city of Jerusalem from the Jebusites and establishes it as the capital of the united Kingdom of Israel. David is important because the Messiah is to come through the line of David.[7]
- 966 BC: Solomon (David's son) builds the first temple in Jerusalem.[8]
- 722 BC: The Assyrians conquer Israel.[9]
- 586 BC: The Babylonians (formerly Babel) destroy the temple and sack the city of Jerusalem.[10]
- 516 BC: The Jewish people return to Jerusalem. The city is rebuilt and the second temple is constructed.[11]
- 332 BC: Alexander the Great conquers Persia; Judea and Jerusalem come under Macedonian rule.[12]
- 198 BC: Judea/Jerusalem is lost to the Seleucids under Antiochus III, who tries to Hellenize the Jews.[13]
- 152 BC: The Maccabean revolt results in the establishment of the Hasmonean kingdom with Jerusalem as its capital.[14]

- 63 BC: Pompey the Great conquers Jerusalem (and the Hasmonean kingdom); Rome installs Herod as a client king.[15]

Yeshua and the Heavenly New Jerusalem

And finally we have arrived at the point in our story of Jerusalem in which the first stage of the protevangelium (the last part of Genesis 3:15, which says Messiah shall bruise the serpent's heel) is fulfilled. Yeshua, the One who would crush the serpent under His heel, is born in nearby Bethlehem. He also will redefine the very meaning of Jerusalem, translating it from a temporal reality into a transcendent, spiritual reality. We see this spoken of in detail in the Book of Revelation. However, this will not happen without destruction and dispersion first.

> Now when *Yeshua* went out and was going away from the Temple, His disciples came up to point out to Him the Temple buildings. "Don't you see all these?" He responded to them. "Amen, I tell you, not one stone will be left here on top of another—every one will be torn down!"
>
> —Matthew 24:1–2

We also see the beginning of a new spiritual reality that replaces the Temple and sacrificial system. Yeshua now becomes the "stone the builders rejected" (Ps. 118:22). First Peter 2:4–5 reveals Yeshua is the "living stone rejected by men" and tells us that "you also, as living stones, are being built up as a spiritual house—a holy priesthood to offer up spiritual sacrifices acceptable to God through Messiah *Yeshua*." First Corinthians 6:19 repeats this imagery: "Or don't you know that your body is a temple of the *Ruach ha-Kodesh*

[Holy Spirit] who is in you, whom you have from God, and that you are not your own?"

These two passages seem to point to the idea that Jerusalem is both a temporal *and* spiritual reality. And the temple is not just a temporal reality, one built of stone; rather, it is built of people, the *ecclesia*, the true followers of Yeshua.

In his letter to the Ephesians, Paul furthers the idea that Jerusalem is both a physical and spiritual reality when he writes that the Gentiles are now brought into the covenant God made with Israel and together we are being built into a dwelling place for God:

> And He came and proclaimed *shalom* to you who were far away and *shalom* to those who were near—for through Him we both have access to the Father by the same *Ruach*. So then you are no longer strangers and foreigners, but you are fellow citizens with God's people and members of God's household. You have been built on the foundation made up of the emissaries and prophets, with Messiah *Yeshua* Himself being the cornerstone. In Him the whole building, being fitted together, is growing into a holy temple for the Lord. In Him, you also are being built together into God's dwelling place in the *Ruach* [Spirit].
>
> —Ephesians 2:17–22

It seems to me that God is desiring to fulfill His plan for both the church and the Jewish people along parallel paths. Both Christians and observant Jews are expecting the coming of the Messiah. One is waiting for His return to complete the work of redemption that began at Calvary; the other is anticipating the coming of King Messiah to establish a Messianic age of peace and prosperity. What many don't understand, however, is that both are waiting for the same Person. And, I believe, we will all behold Him soon!

The Times of the Gentiles: Ancient Times

As mentioned previously, in AD 70 the entire city of Jerusalem was destroyed along with the temple. The Jews who were not killed either were sold into slavery or fled the city. The historian Josephus wrote that the city "was so thoroughly razed to the ground by those that demolished it to its foundations, that nothing was left that could ever persuade visitors that it had once been a place of habitation."[16] His description of the fall of Jerusalem is very similar to the prophecy Yeshua made regarding the utter destruction of the temple in Matthew 24.

In AD 132, around sixty years after the temple's destruction, the remaining Jews in what was now called Palestine (renamed by the Romans) waged another revolt against Rome under the leadership of Shimon Bar-Kokhba, a false messiah who had many followers. However, Rome completely overwhelmed the rebellion, and once again the Jews were scattered throughout the region and beyond in a diaspora (dispersion) that continued for over eighteen hundred years until the establishment of the State of Israel in 1948.[17] In fact, more than 50 percent of the Jewish people still live outside of the land of Israel.[18]

With the temple and city of Jerusalem destroyed and the Jewish people dispersed to the nations, those Jews who did not accept Yeshua as the Messiah now had to redefine themselves in order to survive. They recreated their religious practice to no longer include a temple, priesthood, and sacrificial system. Rabbinic Judaism emerged, entrusting full authority to the rabbis to interpret the meaning of Scripture. At the root was a rejection of the messiahship of Yeshua. The gulf between "church and synagogue" grew, and in the ensuing centuries Satan masterminded one of the most evil plans of all time—turning Gentile Christians against the very seed from which Yeshua had sprung, the very people God chose to proclaim His salvation to the ends of the earth: the people of Israel.

The Jews suffered centuries of persecution following the destruction of the temple by the Romans. Scattered in all directions from their homeland, they carried Jerusalem in their hearts as they wandered throughout the world— to Europe, Asia, and Africa, and eventually North and South America. Those who stayed in the Middle East were subjugated by various invaders, Muslims and the Crusaders, to name just two. Those who made their way to Europe and Asia suffered unimaginable indignities and worse: pogroms (organized massacres) in Russia and ern Europe. And by 1844, there were just a few thousand Jews left in Palestine.

The Times of the Gentiles: Modern Times

In about 1870, the Jewish population in the Middle East began to grow. It wasn't exactly a population explosion, but a number of Jewish families returned to Palestine and began farming there. These pioneers found a land that was largely deserted. There was plenty of land but not much else. Towns were few and far between. Supplies and farming tools had to be brought in from long distances. The Jewish farmers worked long, hard days trying to grow enough food to feed their families. It wasn't easy, but slowly and surely they began to transform the swamps and reestablish a Jewish presence in the Middle East.[19]

At this time, Palestine was under the complete control of the Ottoman Empire. Felix Bovet, a Swiss scholar who spent some time in the region, said the Turks had "turned it [Palestine] into a wasteland in which they seldom dare to tread without fear."[20]

It wasn't until a quarter century later, in 1896, that the modern Zionist movement was born. That was when Theodor Herzl wrote a book called *The Jewish State*. Herzl, who was born in Hungary and attended college in Austria, had encountered a great deal of anti-Semitism during his time in Europe. He was moved to action when he encountered mobs in Paris shouting "Death to the Jews." The Jewish Virtual Library says that Herzl "resolved that there was only one solution: the mass immigration of Jews to a land that they could call their own. . . . Herzl argued that the essence of the Jewish problem was not individual but national. He declared that the Jews could gain acceptance in the world only if they ceased being a national anomaly. The Jews are one people, he said, and their plight could be transformed into a positive force by the establishment of a Jewish state with the consent of the great powers."[21]

Herzl was a journalist, and one of the catalysts for his work on behalf of a Jewish state in the Middle East came when he covered a famous trial that came to be known as the Dreyfus Affair. A French Army officer named Alfred Dreyfus was falsely accused of selling military secrets to the Germans. Dreyfus was a Jew, and because of this he could not get a fair trial. Evidence that could have proved his innocence was suppressed, and fake evidence was introduced to help convict him. Dreyfus spent several years in prison at Devil's Island before being pardoned by the French government and, eventually, completely exonerated. Herzl was horrified by the anti-Semitism that emerged in Dreyfus's trial and saw the frightening implications for all Jews in France and throughout Europe. From that point on, he devoted his life to the creation of a Jewish homeland, becoming known as "the visionary of Zionism."

In 1897 Herzl organized what became known as the World Zionist Organization, which held its first international conference in Basel, Switzerland. He later stated, "In Basel I founded the Jewish state."[22] Unfortunately, he did not live long enough to see his dreams become reality. He died in 1904, at the age of forty-four.

In 1949, after the establishment of Israel, his remains were moved from Vienna to Mount Herzl in Jerusalem.[23]

Now, there was not a universal consensus that the Jews should return to the Middle East. Other plans were proposed. Some suggested British East Africa as the site for a new Jewish state—Uganda, or what is today Kenya, to be more specific. Argentina was also suggested, as was Manchuria. Even Grand Island, New York; and Sitka, Alaska, were considered.[24] Of course, the Jews loudly rejected all of these options. There was only one place that was right for a Jewish state, and that was on the land promised to Abraham almost four thousand years ago.

Thirteen years after Herzl's death, British Foreign Secretary Arthur Balfour wrote the famous Balfour Declaration, a milestone leading to the formation of the modern State of Israel. In a letter to Baron Walter Rothschild intended to be transmitted to the Zionist Federation of Great Britain and Ireland, Balfour wrote:

> His Majesty's Government view with favour the establishment in Palestine of a national home for the Jewish people, and will use their best endeavors to facilitate the achievement of this object, it being clearly understood that nothing shall be done which may prejudice the civil and religious rights of existing non-Jewish communities in Palestine or the rights and political status enjoyed by Jews in any other country.[25]

The letter also stated that the British government was acting in sympathy with "Jewish Zionist aspirations."[26]

Balfour was a Christian who firmly believed that the return of the Jews to Israel was connected to the second coming of Christ.[27] But despite his call for a "national home for the Jewish people" in Palestine, no official action was taken. However, that did not discourage Jews at that time from returning to Palestine in larger and larger numbers.

At first there was a great deal of support for the establishment of a Jewish homeland in the Middle East. But then, as had happened so often before, the tide of public opinion turned against the Jews. Nazi Germany wasn't the only country in the world where Jews were blamed for the economic troubles unleashed by the Great Depression. The world needed a scapegoat, and it found one in the descendants of Abraham. Even Britain, which had produced the Balfour Declaration, turned against the Jews.

In his book *A Durable Peace*, former Israeli Prime Minister Benjamin Netanyahu writes, "Early in 1939, Prime Minister Neville Chamberlain concocted the formula that was to bring 'peace in our time' to the Middle East. His solution to the Arabs' unhappiness with the Balfour Declaration was to abrogate the declaration once and for all. The Chamberlain White Paper of May 1939 was issued four months before the outbreak of World War II and the final countdown to the Holocaust. It decreed that Jewish immigration was to be finally terminated after the entry of another seventy-five thousand Jews, and that Britain would now work to create a 'binational' Arab-Jewish state."[28]

Netanyahu goes on to say, "The extent of British betrayal of the Jews can be understood only in the context of what was happening in Europe in the 1930s and thereafter. Responding to pressure from the Arabs, the British restriction of Jewish immigration (there was no analogous restriction on *Arab* immigration) cut off the routes of escape for Jews trying to flee a burning Europe. Thus, while the Gestapo was conniving to send boatloads of German Jews out onto the high seas to prove that no country wanted them any more than Germany did, the British dutifully turned back every leaking barge that reached Palestine, even firing on several."[29]

In 1942, the British refused passage to Palestine to the ship *Stuma*, which later sank, drowning over seven hundred Jewish refugees from the Holocaust.[30] These were the brutal, unimaginable years, when the Nazis were determined to kill as many Jews as they possibly could. In just seven horrifying and monstrous years, six million Jews were slaughtered, including almost the entire Jewish population of Poland. Before the war the Jewish population of Poland was three million. In 1950, five years after the Holocaust, only forty-five thousand remained.[31]

The battered and traumatized Jews of Europe who survived sought refuge in Palestine after the war. But just when it seemed they could suffer no more, the British, still in charge of Palestine, turned against them and passed laws limiting the number of Jews allowed to immigrate. They blockaded the ports, arrested many Jews who attempted to sneak into the country, and set up internment camps in Cyprus. From 1946 to 1949, it is estimated that over fifty thousand Jews were held in twelve such camps, where many Jews died.[32]

But this only inspired the Jews living in Palestine to do everything in their power to expel the British from the region. Finally, in 1947, the British agreed to leave, and by a vote of the United Nations (UN Resolution 181) Palestine was divided into Jewish and Arab sections.[33] On the one hand, this was a great day for the soon-to-be fledgling Jewish state, but they were also surrounded on all sides by enemies who wanted them wiped off the face of the earth.

And it didn't take long for those enemies to strike. The day after Israel declared statehood on May 14, 1948, its Arab neighbors attacked it from all sides. Outnumbered sixty to one, it seemed certain Israel would fall in defeat—but it didn't. Israel defeated its enemies in a miraculous victory.[34] Any historian or military strategist might have claimed this was impossible—but we know nothing is impossible with God, especially when we are talking about something that was prophesied in Scripture:

> Who has heard such a thing? Who has seen such things? Can a land be born in one day? Can a nation be brought forth at once? For as soon as Zion was in labor, she gave birth to her children.
>
> —Isaiah 66:8

Of course, Satan does not take kindly to defeat, and he has continued his war against the Jewish people and their homeland of Israel to this day.

The Suez War of 1956

Another threat came against Israel in 1956 when Egypt closed the Suez Canal to Israeli ships. The Suez Canal was a major thoroughfare for the movement of cargo and supplies in and out of the region. This was a strategic move on the part of the Egyptians and could have easily been considered an act of war in and of itself. The United Nations responded by ordering the canal opened to all, but Egypt refused to comply.

In fact, Egypt not only refused to comply, but President Nasser also sent scores of terrorists into Israel with this proclamation: "Egypt has decided to dispatch her heroes, the disciples of Pharaoh and the sons of Islam and they will cleanse the land of Palestine.... There will be no peace on Israel's border because we demand vengeance, and vengeance is Israel's death."[35] If that weren't enough, the foreign minister, Muhammad Salah al-Din, insisted, "We shall not be satisfied except by the final obliteration of Israel from the map of the Middle East."[36]

With Israelis being threatened and killed, Israel had to retaliate. To anyone who didn't realize God's plan, this looked like a military impossibility. But in fact, the Israelis quickly defeated the Egyptian army and even pushed far into Egyptian territory—territory they actually returned to Egypt under the urging of President Eisenhower.[37]

Of course, this was during the Cold War, when the Soviet Union poured billions of dollars' worth of weapons into the hands of Israel's enemies. The Soviets encouraged the Arab nations to attack their tiny neighbor not once but four times, and each time God gave Israel the victory!

The Six-Day War

On May 20, 1967, the Defense Minister of Syria proclaimed, "Our forces are now entirely ready...to explode the Zionist presence in the Arab homeland. The Syrian army, with its finger on the trigger, is united...I, as a military man, believe that the time has come to enter into a battle of annihilation."[38] This was followed ten days later with a pronouncement from Egypt's President Nasser that "The armies of Egypt, Jordan, Syria, and Lebanon are poised on the borders of Israel...to face the challenge, while standing behind us are the armies of Iraq, Algeria, Kuwait, Sudan, and the whole Arab nation. This act will astound the world. Today they will know that the Arabs are arranged for battle, the critical hour has arrived. We have reached the stage of serious action and not declarations."[39]

They astounded the world all right with their high and mighty words—until their Arab coalition was defeated in just six days.

But there was something much more significant that happened in this war. It liberated Jerusalem from Jordanian control. And for the first time in nearly two thousand years, Jerusalem was back in Jewish hands. This marked a prophetic shift in history and was a direct fulfillment of Yeshua's revelation in Luke 21:24 that Jerusalem would be trodden down by the Gentiles. The times of the Gentiles were fulfilled.

I believe we have been undergoing a transition since that event took place a half century ago. The time of the Gentiles has been drawing to a close, and this means the end of our age is drawing near. Luke 21:29–33 says: "Then *Yeshua* told them a parable: 'Look at the fig tree and all the trees. As soon as they sprout their leaves, you see it and you know at once that summer is near. So also, when you see these all these things happening, know that the kingdom of God is near. Amen, I tell you, this generation will not pass away until all these things happen. Heaven and earth will pass away, but My words will never pass away.'"

In addition to the fulfillment of the time of the Gentiles, there are additional "signs of the times" that are recorded in Matthew chapter 24. They include:

- **Deception**—"Be careful that no one leads you astray! For many will come in My name, saying, 'I am the Messiah,' and will lead many astray" (vv. 4–5).

- **Wars and conflicts**—"You will hear of wars and rumors of wars. See that you are not alarmed, for this must happen but it is not yet the end. For nation will rise up against nation, and kingdom against kingdom" (vv. 6–7).

- **Natural disasters and famines**—"And there will be famines and earthquakes in various places" (v. 7).

- **Growing persecution against the Jewish people**—"Then they will hand you over to persecution and will kill you. You will be hated by all the nations because of My name" (v. 9).

- **Signs in the heavens**—"The sun will be darkened, and the moon will not give its light and the stars will fall from heaven and the powers of the heavens will be shaken" (v. 29).

- **Return to the days of Noah**—"For just as the days of Noah were, so will be the coming of the Son of Man. For in those days before the flood, they were eating and drinking, marrying and giving in marriage, until the day Noah entered the ark. And they did not understand until the flood came and swept them all away. So shall it be at the coming of the Son of Man" (vv. 37–39).

Ever since Yeshua ascended into heaven, and even during His earthly ministry, people have looked at these signs (of which there have been plenty) and wondered if "the end" was near. It is true, you cannot look at any period of human history and not find one or more of these signs. However, the restoration of Jerusalem after almost twenty centuries of wandering stands alone. One cannot find the sign of the fulfillment of the time of the Gentiles except for the day in which we are living—and that is significant.

We have seen how the serpent Satan has struck evil in the hearts of men time and again to prevent the return of God's chosen people to Jerusalem and the restoration of that great city. Indeed, the enemy has worked overtime to prevent this prophesied restoration of Jerusalem and return of the Jewish people to their homeland. But despite his best efforts, Israel has been restored as a nation and Jerusalem as its capital. Millions of Jewish families who were scattered to the four corners of the earth have now returned to their homeland and are building new lives there.

This is also a fulfillment of the prophecy recorded in Deuteronomy 30:2–3, "And when you and your children return to the Lord your God and obey him with all your heart and with all your soul according to everything I command you today, then the Lord your

God will restore your fortunes and have compassion on you and gather you again from all the nations where he scattered you" (NIV).

God will no longer be known as the God who brought the children of Israel out of Egypt, but as the God who brought His chosen people from the nations of the world back to the land of their fathers.

Rebuilding the Temple?

Another interesting development worth noting is the movement to rebuild a third temple. This topic is at the heart of a great debate among end-times teachers. Some are convinced the temple will be rebuilt before Messiah returns, while others are equally convinced that the temple will be rebuilt after His coming.

A rebuilt temple is very possible because the ninth chapter of Daniel talks about the abomination of desolation being set up in the temple, and Yeshua mentions this same event in Matthew 24:

> So when you see "the abomination of desolation," which was spoken of through Daniel the prophet, standing in the Holy Place (let the reader understand), then those in Judea must flee to the mountains. The one on the roof must not go down to take what is in his house, and the one in the field must not turn back to get his coat. Woe to those who are pregnant and to those who are nursing babies in those days! Pray that your escape will not happen in winter, or on *Shabbat*. For then there will be great trouble, such as has not happened since the beginning of the world until now, nor ever will.
>
> —Matthew 24:15–21

Although this did happen in 167 BC when the holy of holies was desecrated by the king of the Seleucid Empire, Antiochus IV Epiphanes, many believe it will be repeated by the Antichrist before the return of Jesus. If this is the case, the temple can't be desecrated again if it doesn't exist. In other words, in this scenario the temple must be rebuilt. And because the temple site was divinely appointed, it must be built on its original site.

The problem is that today, two Muslim structures—Al Aqsa, a mosque; and the Dome of the Rock, a shrine—are located on the Temple Mount. Some say the third temple can and will be built next to the Dome of the Rock, which most believe is directly over what was once the holy of holies. Others say it must be built exactly where the Dome is now standing. In the introduction to this book, I mentioned the Temple Institute, an ultra-Orthodox organization that is working to rebuild the temple and train priests to serve there. The institute is one of a dozen groups that are working to rebuild the temple and reinstitute sacrifices, and much of its funding comes from Christian prophecy enthusiasts committed to seeing a third temple rebuilt.

The institute's website says that "in keeping with the oppressive 'rules' set by the Wakf (the Muslim authority granted de facto control of the Temple Mount, by the Israeli government, since 1967), we are, under threat of 'expulsion' from the Mount, not allowed to pray, carry any religious objects, or in any way intimate that we are engaged in worship, while on the Mount."[40]

The Muslims who have had control of the Temple Mount for hundreds of years are not going to do an about-face and agree that Israel can build a third temple there, so the situation is quite complicated. In the meantime, the Temple Institute is training priests to serve in the rebuilt temple. Rabbi Yehoshua Friedman, director of the school for priests, says, "The rabbis say that the minimum necessary is 13 priests in the temple in order to carry out the mandatory sacrifices. If you're talking about a fully operating temple, where people bring their own sacrifices, it's a place where hundreds of priests work daily.... The prayer to establish the temple has no meaning if we don't actually prepare for it. Think what would happen if tomorrow you got a functioning temple and don't have priests."[41]

He goes on to explain that some of the laws for the temple have been forgotten over the years, such as how to use incense, how to light the menorah, how to sanctify hands and feet, and how to make sacrifices. "The priests themselves come with requests to learn one topic or another. We are also learning as we go how the course should look. The students are very practical and focused," explains Friedman.[42]

I do want to put to rest the claims that the temple is actually already rebuilt or in the process of being rebuilt. It is not. Nor is the Israeli government or the Israeli public in general supportive of this or even paying much attention to it. However, it is true that these movements to rebuild the temple do exist and they are gaining momentum. And that in and of itself is noteworthy.

In Luke 21, when Yeshua says Jerusalem shall be trodden down by the Gentiles until the times of Gentiles are fulfilled, He is saying that the restoration of Jerusalem and very possibly the rebuilding of the temple are inextricably bound up with His return and His future earthly reign. And while the debate over whether or not a temple will be rebuilt and then defiled before His return rages, it is certain that a temple will be rebuilt during Yeshua's Messianic reign after He returns.

Dry Bones Are Coming to Life

Another incredible prophecy of the restoration of Israel and Jerusalem, or what I refer to as the "physical restoration of Israel," is in Ezekiel 37:1–6, where we find the story about the valley of dry bones. The Spirit of God came upon the prophet Elijah and set him down in the middle of a valley that was full of dry bones. Then the Spirit of God asked him, "Son of man, can these bones live?" Elijah answered, "*ADONAI Elohim*, You know."

God told Elijah to prophesy over the bones:

> Say to them: "Dry bones, hear the word of *ADONAI*!" Thus says *ADONAI Elohim* to these bones: "Behold, I will cause *Ruach* to enter you, so you will live. I will attach tendons to you, bring flesh on you and cover you with skin. Then I will put breath in you. You will live. You will know that I am *ADONAI*."

We know the Jewish people were driven out of their land and scattered to the nations. In Ezekiel 37 the vacated land is described as filled with their bones. But the Lord promises to breathe life into them, put flesh on them, and renew the valley of Israel, bringing them back to their land and to their God, just as He did in the valley of dry bones. The bones not only came together, but they were also covered with flesh, and then God breathed His life-giving Spirit into them, and they stood as a vast army (Ezek. 37:7–10).

> Then He said to me, "Son of man, these bones are the whole house of Israel. Behold, they say: 'Our bones are dried up; our hope is lost; we are cut off—by ourselves.' Therefore prophesy and say to them, thus says *ADONAI Elohim*: 'Behold, I will open your graves. I will bring you up out of your graves, My people. I will bring you back to the land of Israel. You will know that I am *ADONAI*, when I have opened your graves and brought you up out of your graves, My people. I will put My *Ruach* in you and you will live. I will place you in your own land. Then you will know that I, *ADONAI*, have spoken and that I have done it. . . . I will

> set up My Sanctuary among them forever. My dwelling-place will be over them. I will be their God and they will be My people. Then the nations will know that I am *Adonai* who sanctifies Israel, when My Sanctuary is in their midst forever.'"
>
> —Ezekiel 37:11–14, 26–28

When we reach the last chapter of this book, we will discover that the seventh key to unlocking the prophetic mysteries of Israel is to understand that God has promised a new heaven and a new Earth in which all things will be restored to the way God intended them to be. So even though Jerusalem will be restored prior to this time, it will be made even more glorious when all things are fully restored.

The apostle John was on the island of Patmos, exiled for his faith, when God gave him a vision of the New Jerusalem descending from heaven:

> Then [the angel] carried me away in the *Ruach* to a great and high mountain, and he showed me the holy city, Jerusalem, coming down out of heaven from God, having the glory of God—her radiance like a most precious stone, like a jasper, sparkling like crystal. She had a great, high wall, with twelve gates, and above the gates twelve angels. On the gates were inscribed the names of the twelve tribes of *Bnei-Yisrael*—three gates on the east, three gates on the north, three gates on the south, and three gates on the west. And the wall of the city had twelve foundations, and on them the twelve names of the twelve emissaries of the Lamb.
>
> —Revelation 21:10–14

The city was decorated with every kind of precious stone and its street was made of pure gold, transparent as glass. John goes on to say:

> I saw no temple in her, for its Temple is ADONAI *Elohei-Tzva'ot* and the Lamb. And the city has no need for the sun or the moon to shine on it, for the glory of God lights it up, and its lamp is the Lamb. The nations shall walk by its light, and the kings of the earth bring their glory into it. Its gates shall never be shut by day, for there shall be no night there! And they shall bring into it the glory and honor of the nations. And nothing unholy shall ever enter it, nor anyone doing what is detestable or false, but only those written in the Book of Life.
>
> —REVELATION 21:22–27

To sum up what we've talked about in this chapter, with the restoration of Israel in 1948 and Jerusalem reestablished as its capital and brought back under the control of the Jewish people in 1967, the times of the Gentiles have been transitioning to a close. According to my understanding of Bible prophecy, these events had to happen before the Messiah could return and are clear signals of the end of the age. And while we cannot predict the exact time Yeshua will return, these events let us know the time is drawing near.

I can't wait to see the restored Jerusalem. It will be a radiant, magnificent place, a gathering place for all the nations that will worship there during the Feast of Tabernacles:

> Then all the survivors from all the nations that attacked Jerusalem will go up from year to year to worship the King, ADONAI-*Tzva'ot*, and to celebrate *Sukkot*.
>
> —ZECHARIAH 14:16

One day, you will worship in Jerusalem. That is certain. But I invite you to visit now, before Yeshua returns. There is nothing I love more than to introduce Christians to their second home, Israel, and to the City of the Great King, Jerusalem. Consider this your personal invitation to join me on one of our upcoming Jewish Voice Israel tours. I promise you, it will change your life as well as prepare you for thc day you will return during the Millennium.

Chapter 5

KEY FIVE: THE GOSPEL TO THE JEW FIRST

For I am not ashamed of the Good News, for it is the power of God for salvation to everyone who trusts—to the Jew first and also to the Greek.
—Romans 1:16

The woman was shocked when the young man spoke to her. She was a Samaritan. He was a Jew. And everybody knew Jews looked down their noses at Samaritans. They considered them to be half-breeds, mongrels who had thrown away their godly heritage by intermarrying with non-Jews.

The Jews were also incensed that the Samaritans had the temerity to look down on them. They insisted that they had an older, and therefore more accurate, version of the Holy Scriptures and that their Mount Gerizim, not Jerusalem, was sacred to God.

Jews hated the Samaritans so much that when they were traveling from Judea to Galilee, or vice versa, they usually went miles out of their way to avoid setting foot in Samaria. But here was this fellow, apparently going straight through her country and also asking her to draw Him a drink of water from the nearby well. The rest of the story is found in the fourth chapter of the Gospel of John:

> Then the Samaritan woman tells Him, "How is it that You, a Jew, ask me, a Samaritan woman, for a drink?" (For Jewish people don't deal with Samaritans.)
>
> *Yeshua* replied to her, "If you knew the gift of God, and who it is who is saying to you, 'Give Me a drink,' you would have asked Him, and He would have given you living water."
>
> "Sir," the woman tells Him, "You don't have a bucket, and the well is deep. Then from where do You get this living water?"...
>
> *Yeshua* replied to her, "Everyone who drinks from this water will get thirsty again. But whoever drinks of the water that I will give him shall never be thirsty. The water that I give him will become a fountain of water within him, springing up to eternal life!"
>
> "Sir," the woman tells Him, "give me this water, so I won't get thirsty or have to come all the way here to draw water!"
>
> He tells her, "Go call your husband, and then come back here."
>
> "I don't have a husband," the woman replied.
>
> *Yeshua* tells her, "You've said it right, 'I have no husband.' For you've had five husbands, and the man you have now isn't your husband. This you've spoken truthfully!"
>
> "Sir," the woman tells Him, "I see that You are a prophet!

> Our fathers worshiped on this mountain, but you all say that the place where we must worship is in Jerusalem."
>
> *Yeshua* tells her, "Woman, believe Me, an hour is coming when you will worship the Father neither on this mountain nor in Jerusalem. You worship what you do not know; we worship what we know, for salvation is from the Jews. But an hour is coming—it is here now—when the true worshipers will worship the Father in spirit and truth, for the Father is seeking such people as His worshipers. God is Spirit, and those who worship Him must worship in spirit and truth."
>
> The woman tells Him, "I know that Messiah is coming (He who is called the Anointed One.) When He comes, He will explain everything to us."
>
> *Yeshua* tells her, "I—the One speaking to you—I am."
>
> —John 4:9–11, 13–26

What the World Owes the Jews

There are so many lessons to be learned from this passage of Scripture. For example, when the woman asks, "How is it that You, being a Jew, ask me for a drink since I am a Samaritan woman?" we see that Yeshua's ministry will extend beyond just the Jewish people and include Gentiles and even Samaritans (who were even more despised than the Gentiles).

The Jews and the Samaritans were well aware that sin had brought sickness and death into the world. When Yeshua tells the woman about the water He can give her, the water that will make it so she never thirsts again, He is telling her that she too can have eternal life through faith in Him. This is a signal that His Messianic mission goes beyond what the Jews were expecting. Yeshua is more than just the king Messiah who will liberate the Jews from Roman occupation of their land and reestablish the kingdom of Israel. He is the Savior of the world.

But the main thing I want us to take away from this conversation is Yeshua's proclamation that "salvation is from the Jews." From the very first time He spoke to Abraham, God had already chosen Abraham's descendants to be a light to the nations and bring blessing and salvation to the world. But salvation was to be offered to them first and then through them to all the nations of the world.

The world owes the Jewish people a great debt of gratitude. Yeshua came into the world through the Jews, and they will also play a central role in His return. Any discussion of the last days is incomplete if it doesn't give a prominent role to Israel and the Jewish people.

It is only because of what Yeshua, a Jew, accomplished when He suffered and died on the cross on our behalf that God sees us as holy, set apart, sanctified, and pure. This is a wonderful promise of the new covenant—a promise that was originally given to Israel alone but that Gentiles receive by an engrafting into God's family through faith in Yeshua. It is through this engrafting that Gentiles become partakers in all the promises and blessings of God.

Paul says the gospel is to the Jew first (Rom. 1:16) because all the promises of God were first given to the Jews. Yeshua the Messiah came as a Jew, born of Jewish parents in a Jewish land, and followed the Jewish customs and practices. His disciples were all Jews, and as we've already seen, His earthly ministry was devoted to His own people. He fulfilled the prophecies written by Jewish men in the Jewish Scriptures. What could be more Jewish than to believe in such a Messiah?

John 3:16 says God so loved the world that He gave His one and only Son for all of mankind—Jews and Gentiles alike. But His earthly ministry—His miracles, healings, and teachings—were given to and for the Jewish people. This is very important to understand—the promises and blessings of the new covenant were given to the Jew first, and then, some thirty years later, were opened to the Gentiles.

Thus, the fifth key to unlocking the prophetic mysteries of Israel is to understand that the gospel is to the Jew first, and this precedent remains in effect today. In fact, it is the key that unlocks the gospel's growth to the nations. When we grasp the truth that every Gentile who has received Jesus as Lord and Savior heard the gospel because of the faithfulness of those original Jewish disciples who took the gospel to the ends of the earth, we then realize what a great debt of gratitude we owe to the Jewish people.

The Gospel to the Nations

In my book *A Rabbi Looks at the Last Days*, I told of how God called me to move to Russia to share the good news of the Messiah with the Jewish people there. It was a truly amazing time in my life, and if you haven't yet read that book, I invite you to do so. There is so much I'd like to share with you regarding those years in Russia, but, as I said, much of it is already recorded in my previous book.

One of the stories I related had to do with an experience I had while flying from the former Soviet Union to a speaking engagement in Uppsala, Sweden. On the airplane as I was reading Matthew 24, which talks about the Messiah's return from heaven in the last days, the Holy Spirit drew my attention to a single word in verse 14: "nations."

This verse says that the gospel must be proclaimed to all nations before Yeshua's return. Now, I knew both the Hebrew and Greek translations for this word. In Hebrew, *nations* is *goy* (Gentiles), and *goyum* means "people of the nations." The Greek word for *nations* is *ethnos*, from which we derive the word *ethnic*.

Whenever I read this passage of Scripture previously, I thought of nations as landmasses set apart by geopolitical boundaries established by man. Yet on that flight I realized the word used in this verse literally means "race," "tribe," or, in today's vernacular, "people group" or "ethnic group."[1]

As we have already discussed, the Jewish people have been scattered all over the world. It is rare to find a country without at least some Jews. And the same is true of many other ethnicities. In nearly every nation on Earth you will find a number of distinct people groups. Think of the United States, where there are millions of people of African and Hispanic descent, plus Americans from China, Korea, Vietnam, Ireland, Britain—people from every nation on Earth.

When Jesus said the gospel of the kingdom must be preached to every *ethnos*, He was not saying we had to reach only geopolitical countries. He was saying we had to reach the distinct ethnic groups that live within those countries. This is a great calling for us!

When this is coupled with what Paul tells us in Romans 1:16, that the gospel is "to the Jew first" and then to the nations, we see the priority of taking the gospel to every community in every country where the Jewish people have been scattered. In my mind, this is the missing link in world missions. Reaching the Jewish people is a vitally important key to reaching the nations for Yeshua.

In Romans 11:11–15 we are told that Israel's rejection of Jesus as their Messiah has now caused the gospel to go to the nations (*ethnos*). What a blessing this is for those who were not born Jewish. But if that was a blessing, what greater blessing is in store when the Jews come back to God by recognizing Yeshua is their promised Messiah!

Paul called himself "the apostle to the Gentiles," and it's easy to see why. He traveled throughout the entire known world to spread the good news of the Messiah, Jesus. Even so, everywhere Paul went, he demonstrated this precedent that the gospel was to the Jew first. A careful reading through the Book of Acts will show that whenever Paul went into a new community, the first thing he did was preach the gospel in the local synagogue. Following are some examples:

> Immediately, something like scales fell from Saul's eyes, and he regained his sight. Then he got up and was immersed; and when he had taken food, he was strengthened. Now for several days, he was with the disciples in Damascus. Immediately he began proclaiming *Yeshua* in the synagogues, saying, "He is *Ben-Elohim*."
>
> —Acts 9:18–20

> When they arrived at Salamis, they began to proclaim the word of God in the Jewish synagogues. They also had John as a helper.
>
> —Acts 13:5

> Setting sail from Paphos, Paul's company came to Perga in Pamphylia. John left them and returned to Jerusalem. But they passed on from Perga and came to Antioch of Pisidia. Entering the synagogue on the *Shabbat*, they sat down. After the reading of the *Torah* and the Prophets, the synagogue leaders sent to them, saying, "Brothers, if you have any word of encouragement for the people, speak."
>
> —Acts 13:13–15

> Now in Iconium, the same thing happened—they entered as usual into the Jewish synagogue and spoke in such a way that a large number of Jewish and Greek people believed.
>
> —Acts 14:1

> After passing through Amphipolis and Apollonia, they came to Thessalonica, where there was a Jewish synagogue. As was his custom, Paul went to the Jewish people; and for three *Shabbatot*, he debated the Scriptures with them. He opened them and gave evidence that Messiah had to suffer and rise from the dead, saying, "This *Yeshua*, whom I declare to you, is the Messiah."
>
> —ACTS 17:1–3

OUR DEBT TO THE JEWS

In the early chapters of this book, we spent some time talking about how the Jewish people have suffered at the hands of those who called themselves Christians. This is truly ironic since the Scriptures are so clear that salvation came through the Jews!

You must understand that because I am a Jew myself, I find it a bit difficult to talk this way. The last thing I want you to think is that I feel I am in any way superior. I'm not. Nor do I believe God loves the Jewish people more than He loves Gentiles. Yet in His sovereignty, He has chosen the Jewish people as a special nation, and He has remained faithful to that election. As we read in Romans 11:29 concerning Israel as a people, "for the gifts and the calling of God are irrevocable."

God knows that I have been called names and sneered at because I'm Jewish. I've also been treated with disdain and rejected for my faith in Yeshua. That goes with the territory. I'm simply trying to show you what I see clearly in Scripture because I believe many Christians have never been taught these simple truths and they do matter.

An Amazing Statement From the Apostle Paul

Romans chapters 9 through 11 provide the clearest and most comprehensive teaching in the New Testament concerning the Jewish people and their destiny. Paul starts off in Romans 9:1 with what seems to be an amazing statement in light of the fact that he is writing to Gentile Christians, not Jews: "I am not lying," he says, assuring his audience that his conscience is clear.

Let's stop there for a minute. I find this astounding. If this letter was being read out loud, I can imagine someone calling out, "Wait a minute. Would you please read that part again?" After all, this is Paul writing—a man of great stature known for His unyielding service to God. How could anyone possibly think Paul was lying? Why would he even say this?

Every time I read this passage, I think of someone testifying in a court of law, putting his hand on the Bible and swearing to tell the truth, the whole truth, and nothing but the truth, "so help me God." Why do they need to do this? Because the testimony they bring could save someone's life. Or it could condemn someone to a life sentence or even to death. So it had better be absolutely true. Perhaps Paul is pledging an oath before God because what he is about to declare is of such great import:

> My sorrow is great and the anguish in my heart unending. For I would pray that I myself were cursed, banished from Messiah for the sake of my people—my own flesh and blood, who are Israelites. To them belong the adoption and the glory and the covenants and the giving of the *Torah* and the Temple service and the promises. To them belong

> the patriarchs—and from them, according to the flesh, the Messiah, who is over all, God, blessed forever.
>
> —ROMANS 9:2–5

Let's look closely at why this passage is so astounding. First of all, Paul has been called to preach the gospel to the Gentiles. In fact, he identifies himself in his epistles as an "apostle to the Gentiles" (Rom. 11:13; Gal. 2:8, NIV). And yet here he is speaking to Gentile believers and telling them he would do anything—even give up his own salvation—to bring about the salvation of his own people, the people of Israel. In other words, he would be willing to give up his eternity with the Lord, but for his Jewish brethren, not for the Gentiles. It seems to me that if he wanted to endear himself to the Romans, he would have said something like, "I want you to know that my heart aches for Romans who don't yet have a relationship with God. I'd give everything I have, including my salvation, to see you Romans saved." But that's not what Paul does. Instead, he tells them how much he loves his unbelieving Jewish kinsmen.

The second thing I find remarkable is Paul's statement that he was willing to give up not just his *life*, but his *eternal* life for the sake of his people. Here is a man who had actually been to heaven (2 Cor. 12:2–4), who had experienced its glory, who had devoted his life to helping people get there. He knew the riches of heaven better than most of us. He also grasped the horrors of hell. Yet he says he would be willing to give it all up and face an eternity in hell, separated from God, for their salvation. Incredible!

Now, I've had some wonderful times with God. I've had some visions, deep revelations, and amazing encounters with God. I know the absolutely exhilarating feeling that comes from being in the Lord's presence. On the other hand, I've never been to heaven, so I can only imagine what a wonderful experience that would be. What I can't imagine is loving someone enough to say, "I've been to heaven, and it's absolutely wonderful, but I'm willing not to ever see it again—for your sake."

What incredible love and sacrifice—and for Paul it is also an amazing act of forgiveness. That's the third reason I think this statement is so astounding. Think of all the times Paul had been beaten, stoned, imprisoned, and threatened by his fellow Jews. Yet he still says he would give up his own salvation for the very ones who rejected and hurt him.

I can't honestly tell you that I would give up my salvation for the sake of my family members who aren't yet saved. After all, we're talking about eternity. I can say by the grace of God that I'd be willing to give up my life here on Earth, but that's because I know that as soon as I breathed my last, I would be present with the Lord. How on earth could Paul say such a thing? I believe there are a few reasons.

1. He was expressing God's heart.

I propose to you that when Paul said he would be willing to give up his very salvation for his countrymen, he was expressing the very heart of God Himself. God is saying through Paul, "These people are the apple of My eye. I long for them to return to Me and would be willing to lay down everything for them—and for the rest of the world—including my one and only Son. But first for these, My people. The gospel is first for them." This is the very heart of God concerning the restoration of Israel.

As I mentioned earlier, I believe the parable of the prodigal son is applicable to Israel. The Father is longing for His prodigal son to return. He is longing for the nation He called to be a royal priesthood to return to Him and to their calling.

2. He understood that God is preserving Israel "until."

Paul understood that God is preserving Israel "until." *Until* is a little word, but it's very important with regard to Scripture. God has an "until" concerning Israel. He preserves them until they come into their ultimate destiny, which is spoken of in Jeremiah 31:33–34, the new covenant, where their sins are forgiven; they all know God, from the least to the greatest; they have a spirit of adoption so they can cry, "Abba, Father"; and the law is taken off stone and placed within their hearts and on their minds. That is His destiny for Israel. It is God's plan for the Jewish people. It is a plan God has brought you into by His grace.

3. Paul wanted the Gentiles to share his burden.

It's interesting to me that Paul shared what must have been the deepest truth of his heart with a Gentile audience. I can only surmise that he understood, in a far greater way than the church does today, what the restoration of Israel means in God's plan as well as to the church and the world. It is something quite profound. But I am getting ahead of myself. I'll come back to this point in the next chapter.

I believe another reason Paul was sharing his heart with the Romans in such an open and intimate way is that he wanted them to share his burden for his people, Israel. This is because every Gentile believer is supposed to play a role in the salvation of Israel. But how can they take part if they don't know how important it is or understand that God is calling them to participate?

4. He knew Israel's "stumble" would be only temporary.

In the eleventh chapter of Romans, Paul explains that God is not finished with the Jewish people. He hasn't rejected or replaced the Jewish people.

> I say then, God has not rejected His people, has He? May it never be! For I too am an Israelite, of the seed of Abraham, of the tribe of Benjamin. God has not rejected His people whom He knew beforehand. Or do you not know what the Scripture says about Elijah, how he pleads with God against Israel? "*ADONAI*, they have killed your prophets, they have destroyed your altars; I alone am left, and they are seeking my life." But what is the divine response to him? "I have kept for Myself seven thousand men who have not bowed the knee to Baal." So in the same way also at this present time there has come to be a remnant according to God's gracious choice.
>
> —ROMANS 11:1–5

Paul begins Romans 11 by pointing to himself, saying, "I'm an Israelite. I'm a Jew, but I also know my Messiah. I'm saved. I'm proof that God is not finished with His people. If He was, I wouldn't be writing you."

Paul goes on to say in Romans 11:11–12: "I say then, they did not stumble so as to fall, did they? May it never be! But by their false step salvation has come to the Gentiles, to provoke Israel to jealousy. Now if their transgression leads to riches for the world, and their loss riches for the Gentiles, then how much more their fullness!"

Most of us know what it's like to stumble and fall. Most of my life, I've lived in homes with two floors, and I admit that there are times when I've tripped and stumbled on the stairs. But after I fell, I didn't lie there. It hurt, but it wasn't the end of me. I remember one time when I was visiting friends in Odessa, Ukraine, I slipped and completely went head over heels. If I hadn't managed to grab the railing at the last moment, I might have been seriously injured—or even killed. It took me a few minutes to get back on my feet, and when I did, I was in pain and realized I had pulled my shoulder out of joint. Even now, more than twenty years later, occasional pain will run through my right shoulder from that stumble. And when that happens, I always remember that day in Odessa and thank God I didn't wind up paralyzed or dead—that I didn't fall beyond recovery.

Paul says that although the Israelites stumbled, they did not stumble beyond recovery. As a nation, God's chosen people missed the Messiah, but only for a season. There will come a day when they will recover and receive Him as their own.

Let me say it again: God is not finished with the Jewish people! There is a remnant who are saved by grace. In fact, most believe that "remnant" today is larger than at any other time in history besides, perhaps, the first century. In fact, I've heard it said that more Jewish people have come to know Yeshua in the last forty years than in the previous nineteen hundred years combined.

PROVOKING THE JEWS TO JEALOUSY

Meanwhile, through their temporary fall, God has caused the gospel to go to the Gentiles. Paul goes on to say that along with the gospel, the Gentiles have been given a heavy responsibility. They have been called into the kingdom with a very specific purpose: to provoke the Jews to jealousy.

What does that mean? It means that you possess something they don't have and they want it. That "something" in this case is the love of God. It's the peace that passes understanding that comes from a personal relationship with the Creator of the universe.

Paul is speaking of the jealousy that arises when your Jewish friends see you living a peace-filled, purposeful life because you have a personal relationship with the living God. It's a jealousy that comes when they see that you have a sense of destiny and that you know with certainty where you're going after you die.

You provoke Jewish people to jealousy as you go through

uncertain times like these with a calm assurance that despite everything you see—the terrorism, the crime, the moral decay, the war against everything that seems to be good and decent—everything is still under God's control and will turn out exactly the way He wants it to.

When your Jewish friend or coworker sees these things, he or she may think, "Wait a minute. I'm supposed to be one of the chosen people. How is it that they have such a close relationship with my God, and I don't even know what my own Scriptures say?" Those of us who have accepted Yeshua as our Messiah and Savior, whether we are Jews or Gentiles by birth, should be living in such a way that it makes all unbelievers want to have what we have. The Scriptures tell us that the Jewish people seek after a sign. And that sign, that wonder, that miracle is supposed to come through us because we have a living relationship with the God of Abraham and the Jewish Messiah, Yeshua.

I like the way Derek Leman puts it in his book *The World to Come*. Leman, who like me is a Messianic rabbi says, "What God loves he cares for. His own image and likeness is found in every family in the earth. Love for the older brother does not remove love for the younger. Rather, by prospering the older brother, God is bringing the younger brother blessing as well."[2]

He goes on to explain, "So far, the story since Yeshua's day has been more one of the younger brother receiving the blessing. Countless millions of Gentiles have been touched by God's forgiving love. The older brother brought the scriptures and the Messiah to the younger. All over the world, the blessing of the younger brother can be seen. Chinese wheat farmers know the God of Israel and so do Botswanan bushmen. The older brother right now is in need of the younger. Israel is largely in unbelief while a good portion of the nations believe."[3]

GOD LOVES THE NATIONS

Although God chose the Jews to be His people, set apart for His glory, it has always been His plan that the Jewish people would be a light to the nations, bringing God's love to Gentiles everywhere. God has always cared about the salvation of the entire world. But He chose the Jewish people to be the original carriers of that salvation and redemption. Consider these verses:

> Let the peoples praise You, O God. Let all the peoples praise You. Let the nations be glad and sing for joy, for You will judge the peoples fairly, and guide the nations on the earth. Let the peoples praise You, O God. Let all the peoples praise You.
>
> —PSALM 67:4–6

> It will come to pass in the last days that the mountain of *ADONAI*'s House will stand firm as head of the mountains and will be exalted above the hills. So all nations will flow to it. Then many peoples will go and say: "Come, let us go up to the mountain of *ADONAI*, to the House of the God of Jacob! Then He will teach us His ways, and we will walk in His paths." For *Torah* will go forth from Zion and the word of *ADONAI* from Jerusalem.
>
> —ISAIAH 2:2–3

> I, *ADONAI*, called You in righteousness, I will take hold of Your hand, I will keep You and give You as a covenant to the people, as a light to the nations, by opening blind eyes, bringing prisoners out of the dungeon, and those sitting in darkness out of the prison house.
>
> —ISAIAH 42:6–7

There are many verses that refer to Israel's role to proclaim God's glory and authority throughout the world. This is the principle found in Romans 1:16—"to the Jew first, and also to the Greek."

Derek Leman writes, "The grandeur of all humankind is a teaching of the Bible. God's love has never been limited to one group within humanity. Rather, through one group, Israel, God's love enters the world in a tangible way; through prophets, apostles and ultimately through Messiah.... God will recover and redeem all that he loves, both Israel and the nations.... In that day, 'Adonai will be king over the whole world. On that day Adonai will be the only one, and his name will be the only name.'"[4]

My Search for Truth

From the time I was knee-high, I knew there was a God. I knew there must be more than I was learning in school and synagogue. I learned about Moses. I learned about Abraham. I learned about the God who performed great miracles back in our history but was now too distant for us to communicate with.

Most Jewish people don't even pronounce the name of God. We say "*Adonai*," which means, "Sir." We refer to God as *HaShem*, which is literally "The Name." A Jewish person who is devout will not even write the name of God because it is too holy. This is why you may see His name written G-d or L-rd in some Jewish literature. And while there is a great reverence for God's holiness, He is also distant and unapproachable in a personal sense.

I dared to ask, Where is the God who spoke to Abraham? Where is the God who appeared to Moses? One teacher referred to how God appeared to Moses as a burning bush. But how does one have a relationship with a burning bush?

I remember asking this teacher, "What does it mean that we are the chosen people?" I'll never forget her answer. "We were chosen to be persecuted," she replied. I remember thinking, "Well, if that's the case, I have no interest in being Jewish!"

I also wanted to know what happened after we died. I remember on "Ask the Rabbi Day," I went to the rabbi and asked him, "What happens when we die?" I'll never forgot his answer: "We're climbing a mountain and can only see the trees ahead. Only God sees over the top. But when we get to the top, then we will see what lies beyond." He had no idea what happens when a person dies.

I had no answers either. I learned a lot about God and about Jewish history as a youth but never learned how to know God. Then at age twenty I was confronted with the reality of my sin and separation from God one Saturday night at a Bible study I attended with a friend. I prayed a simple prayer, and afterward I somehow felt different. In the months that followed, I began to read the Bible, and slowly my life was changed.

I now know the prayer I prayed that night was a confession of the faith that was in my heart, and I was saved. As we are told in Romans 10:9–10: "For if you confess with your mouth that *Yeshua* is Lord, and believe in your heart that God raised Him from the dead, you will be saved. For with the heart it is believed for righteousness, and with the mouth it is confessed for salvation." Now, as it was with Paul, my heart's desire and prayer for Israel is that they might be saved (Rom. 10:1).

JEWS DO NOT BELIEVE IN JESUS

Although there is much debate about what a good Jew believes, there is great unity within the Jewish community on what Jews do not believe. And what Jews do not believe in—or rather whom Jews do not believe in—is Jesus. This is the result of an almost two-thousand-year legacy of persecution in His name that believers must overcome. We have to show our Jewish friends and neighbors that there is a major difference between those who are true, Bible-believing Christians and those who call themselves Christians but according to the Bible are not. We are warned in the Ten Commandments against taking the name of God in vain. That is exactly what many do who claim to be Christians but show by their actions that they are not. Those of us who truly belong to Yeshua are called to model His love to the world.

Just before His arrest and crucifixion, Yeshua told His disciples, "This is My commandment, that you love one another just as I have loved you" (John 15:12). Before my personal encounter with Yeshua, I was searching for God in all the wrong places. I had zeal but not according to knowledge. I was searching for the meaning and purpose of my life, so I became involved in all kinds of cults and the occult. I was in Hare Krishna for a while, chanting. Oddly enough, it is possible to be a Hare Krishna and still be considered a "good Jew." But this phase came to an end for me when I had been involved long enough to find out that I needed to become a vegetarian and shave my head. As one who loves meat and who was already losing his hair, I said, "You're not touching one hair on this head."

After that, I tried all kinds of bizarre things until ultimately God apprehended me and transformed my life. And by the way, it is no coincidence that the cults and the occult are disproportionately filled with Jewish people. The Bible says in Romans 10:2 that they have a zeal for God, but not according to knowledge, just as it was with me.

Paul begins Romans chapter 10 by reiterating his heart for his own people, Israel. He writes, "Brothers and sisters, my heart's desire and my prayer to God for Israel is for their salvation." He then goes on to talk about God's plan for their salvation and just how easy it is for Jewish people to be saved. He says all they have to do is call upon the name of the Lord. That's it. But they can't believe in the Lord and call upon His name if they have never heard about Him. They can't believe unless someone goes to them and tells them.

Paul tells us in Romans 10:17, "So faith comes from hearing, and hearing by the word of Messiah." Although this truth can be applied to all people, in context Paul is talking about the salvation of the Jewish people and how simple it is for them to believe. All they need to do is hear. Sadly, this context is often overlooked or ignored completely by Bible expositors.

Every individual who has made Yeshua Lord of his or her life should be praying for the salvation of the Jewish people. If you don't know any Jewish people personally, pray that the Lord brings a Jewish person into your life, and in the meantime pray for the Jewish people in general. And if you do have Jewish friends, don't shy away from sharing your faith with them. Of course, be tactful and wait for the right timing. Don't shove the gospel down their throats, but share your testimony with them. Tell them how the God of Israel changed your life. Every believer has a role to play in God's plan for the Jewish people. When the Jewish people turn their hearts toward Messiah, Israel will be restored, and we will move another major step toward His return.

A Great End-Times Revival Is Coming

You may remember Yeshua's parable in which He taught that the kingdom of heaven may start off like the tiniest of seeds. It seems insignificant and small at first. It may grow slowly. But it will keep growing until it "becomes like a tree, so that the birds of the air come and nest in its branches" (Matt. 13:32).

Perhaps you've heard the story of the Chinese bamboo tree. It all begins with the planting of a tiny seed. For the first year after you plant it, you have to water it regularly, fertilize it, cultivate it to keep the weeds away—and nothing happens. The second year is a repeat of the first. Two more years go by and nothing at all seems to be happening. For all you know, the seed died shortly after you planted it. Even so, you don't give up. You keep watering, fertilizing, and clearing weeds.

And then, in year five, that little seed suddenly explodes into action. In a matter of six weeks, that bamboo tree shoots up ninety feet.

I believe this is a good analogy of what is about to take place among the Jewish people all over the world, including in Israel. The seeds of salvation were first planted there almost two thousand years ago. But they are just now getting ready to once again erupt into action.

I can almost feel it. It's like there is a volcano rumbling beneath our feet. I believe that over the next few years we will see growing numbers of Jewish people find their Messiah. Even now the Lord is pouring out His Spirit upon them. Many are having dreams and visions. Young and old, the blindness is coming off the eyes of many. The good news began with the Jewish people, and in the same way it will conclude with Jewish people in the end times.

Yes, the gospel is still to the Jew first. It is the missing key of missiology. And when this precedent is followed, it will release greater openness to the gospel in the nations.

Chapter 6

KEY SIX: BRINGING LIFE FROM THE DEAD

For if their [the Jews'] rejection [of the Messiah] leads to the reconciliation of the world, what will their acceptance be but life from the dead?

—Romans 11:15

There was only one thing that could have made Jeni Stepien's wedding day more perfect: her father could have been there to walk her down the aisle. Tragically, her father was murdered—shot down during an armed robbery—ten years earlier.

Nothing could have made up for the loss of her daddy. Still, some good came out of Michael Stepien's death. Jeni's father was an organ donor. His heart helped to save the life of a man named

Arthur Thomas. In a very real way, Thomas received life from the dead. Without the heart he received from Jeni's dad, he most certainly would have died. He had been diagnosed with ventricular tachycardia sixteen years earlier, and time was running out.

In the decade after Thomas's heart transplant, Jeni and her family stayed in touch with him. They exchanged letters, gifts, and phone calls. Despite the friendship that developed between them, Thomas was shocked when he received an important and unexpected request from Jeni—"Will you walk me down the aisle?"[1]

His answer was that he'd be happy to do so. It wasn't until the day before Jeni's wedding that she met face-to-face with the man who had been saved by her father's heart. What an emotional moment it was when Jeni walked down the aisle arm-in-arm with the man who had her father's heart beating inside him. It's rare to have a wedding without tears, and there was no shortage of them on this big day. Jeni said, "It's just like having my dad here and better because we get to share this story with people and other people see that organ donors do matter."[2] She later wrote on Facebook, "It truly was the best day of MY ENTIRE LIFE! To be able to bring my dad home and have him at my wedding was an absolute dream COME TRUE!"[3]

Her sister, Michelle, said, "Just hugging him made me feel like I was close to my dad again which on this day was perfect. It was what I needed."[4] Although Thomas has a daughter of his own, she is not yet married, and Jeni Stepien is the first woman he's had the honor of walking down the aisle.[5]

What does this have to do with the fulfillment of biblical prophecy? Quite a bit, actually.

First of all, as we've already seen, God says a day is coming when He will put a new heart inside His people—a stronger, better heart; a heart of flesh upon which is written His Torah, His law. He also tells us, through the apostle Paul, that a day is coming when the world will experience *life from the dead*. How will this happen, and when? The answer lies in a unique interconnection found in Romans 11:11–15:

> I say then, they did not stumble so as to fall, did they? May it never be! But by their false step salvation has come to the Gentiles, to provoke Israel to jealousy. Now if their transgression leads to riches for the world, and their loss riches for the Gentiles, then how much more their fullness! But I am speaking to you who are Gentiles. Insofar as I am an emissary to the Gentiles, I spotlight my ministry if somehow I might provoke to jealousy my own flesh and blood and save some of them. For if their rejection leads to the reconciliation of the world, what will their acceptance be but life from the dead?

Here we are told that there is relationship between the rejection of Yeshua by Israel and the gospel opening up to the nations. As a result of Israel's rejection of Messiah, the gospel has now gone to the Gentiles. This relates back to the previous chapter where I talked about the gospel being to the Jew first and the fact that Yeshua's entire early ministry was to His own people. It had to happen this way because this is God's divine order. But in the same way Israel's rejection of the gospel brought a particular result, so will its acceptance of the good news. Their rejection released the gospel to go to the other nations of the world, but their acceptance releases something far greater—"life from the dead."

Thus the sixth key to unlocking the prophetic mysteries of Israel and understanding Israel's role in end-time prophecy is to understand that when Israel accepts Jesus as their Messiah, it will release life from the dead upon all the nations of the earth.

Faith Among the Jews

As we discussed in chapter 3, over the last nineteen hundred-plus years, there has always been a remnant of Jews who believed in Jesus. Don't forget, all the first followers of Yeshua were Jewish, and we know from historians that the number of followers was in the tens of thousands.

So while many Jews in the time of Yeshua did become believers and there has always been this remnant, it has been a minority. The vast majority of Jewish people have not accepted Yeshua over the centuries, and the gatekeepers of Judaism, the rabbis, have rejected His claim of messiahship. It's interesting to me that during Yeshua's time on Earth, opposition to Him came almost entirely from the religious leaders. Today, it's still the leaders who are most opposed to Him.

Most did eventually reject Yeshua because they were uneducated in the Scriptures and followed the direction of their spiritual leaders. Still, it was in fulfillment of God's divine plan that Jesus and His disciples walked and taught exclusively among the Jewish people for three years. When Jesus sent seventy of His disciples out to heal the sick and preach the good news of the kingdom, He told them to go only to the lost sheep of the house of Israel (Matt. 10:6). When a Canaanite woman begged Jesus to heal her daughter, He said, "I was sent only to the lost sheep of the house of Israel" (Matt. 15:24). In using this metaphor, He was most likely referring to Jeremiah 50:6, which says, "My people have been lost sheep. Their shepherds led them astray. Turning around in the mountains, they went from mountain to hill, and forgot their resting place."

It was not until shortly before His arrest and crucifixion that He announced, "I am the Good Shepherd. I know My own and My own know Me, just as the Father knows Me and I know the Father. And I lay down My life for the sheep. I have other sheep that are not from this fold; those also I must lead, and they will listen to My voice. So there shall be one flock, one Shepherd" (John 10:14–16).

In other words, it was only after Yeshua had poured Himself out completely to reach the Jewish people that the doors swung wide to allow people from every nation to enter God's kingdom. In the Book of Revelation, John gives this glorious prophecy of people from all over the world—Jews and non-Jews alike—praising God together:

> After these things I looked, and behold, a vast multitude that no one could count—from every nation and all tribes and peoples and tongues—was standing before the throne and before the Lamb. They were clothed in white robes, with palm branches in their hands and crying out with a loud voice, saying, "Salvation belongs to our God, who sits on the throne, and to the Lamb!"
>
> —Revelation 7:9–10

God So Loved the World

As we've already seen, those who bless Israel will be blessed and those who curse Israel will be cursed. This is as true for nations as it is for individuals.

If you want to see an outpouring of the Spirit on the nations of the world, pray for the salvation of Israel. When Israel turns to the Messiah, "life from the dead" will flow into every corner of the globe! This will be the start of the biggest revival in history. Imagine the soul-winning crusades of Billy Graham multiplied many times over. It will be far greater than the all the revivals led by all the great evangelists of history—Charles Spurgeon, Dwight L. Moody, Charles Finney, John Wesley, Jonathan Edwards, Billy Sunday, and everyone else you can think of—combined! It will be the great outpouring spoken of in Joel 3:1: "I will pour out My *Ruach* [Spirit] on all flesh: your sons and daughters will prophesy, your old men will dream dreams, your young men will see visions."

I've prayed and meditated long and hard about what this phrase means, and I'm quite certain that "life from the dead" has to do with finishing the work of atonement that restores the earth to the way it was always meant to be—the condition it was in before the fall of man. We are all under a death sentence because of Adam and Eve's sin. But when life comes from the dead, we will all be set free!

I know of only two people in all of history who never died: Enoch and Elijah. Enoch walked with God and was no more because God took him, and Elijah was taken to heaven in a fiery chariot. Everyone else has died. All the apostles died. George Washington and Abraham Lincoln died. Elvis Presley and Marilyn Monroe died, as did Mother Teresa and Nelson Mandela. Two of the Beatles are dead.

Death is the great equalizer. No one can escape death, and no one can take their money and possessions with them when they die. Think of the ancient pharaohs who tried to take their riches with them into the next world. Their tombs were filled with gold and silver and precious possessions of all kinds. Thousands of years later, when their tombs were opened, the riches were still here in this world. They were of no use in the hereafter. We come into this world empty handed, and we go out of it the same way.

But good news is on the way! Death is about to be swallowed up in victory. When life comes from death, we will be living in a world that operates as it was originally intended to—a world without sickness, pain, death, or suffering of any kind.

A World Without Death

Imagine opening your newspaper in the morning and finding nothing in it that makes you feel sad or angry. Nothing about terrorist attacks, deadly earthquakes, unthinkable crimes, or terrible accidents. The good news is that this isn't a fantasy dreamed up by some Hollywood screenwriter. It is what God has planned for His people on His planet. It's about to become a reality, and you and I can help make it happen.

How? I can tell you one way. We can help take the gospel to Jewish people all over the world so they can hear, believe, and be saved. When that occurs, Romans 11:15 will come to pass and life will come from the dead.

Yeshua had some important words to say about life coming from the dead. Shortly before His arrest, trial, and execution, He told His disciples, "Very truly I tell you, unless a kernel of wheat falls to the ground and dies, it remains only a single seed. But if it dies, it produces many seeds. Anyone who loves their life will lose it, while anyone who hates their life in this world will keep it for eternal life. Whoever serves me must follow me; and where I am, my servant also will be. My Father will honor the one who serves me" (John 12:24–26, NIV). In Matthew 16:25 He says, "whoever wants to save their life will lose it, but whoever loses their life for me will find it" (NIV).

When Jesus went to the cross, Satan thought he had won a final victory over God. But he was wrong. Every painful lash Yeshua endured, every punch from jeering Roman soldiers, every excruciating blow that drove the nails further into His hands and feet was bringing not defeat but victory over sin and death. It is only when we die to self that the Spirit of God can live within us and make Himself known through us.

During His last Passover with His disciples, Yeshua told them,

"I tell you the truth, it is to your advantage that I go away! For if I do not go away, the Helper will not come to you; but if I go, I will send Him to you" (John 16:7). When Yeshua talked about "going away," He was talking about dying. Or at least that's part of what He was talking about. If He did not die, there would have been no resurrection. If there was no resurrection, there would have been no ascension to the right hand of God. And finally, if Yeshua had not given up His life on the cross, the Holy Spirit would not have come into the world to guide us, and we would all be left on our own to struggle through the darkness.

In many ways, Yeshua's crucifixion was the saddest and most tragic event ever to occur. But in many other ways, it was one of the happiest moments in all history. Of course, I absolutely hate that He had to suffer. It breaks my heart when I think of Him being beaten until He was almost dead and then being nailed to that cross. I shudder to think of Him hanging there in agony, struggling for every breath, and it's even worse to think that my sins played a part in putting Him there. But at the same time, I am so deeply grateful that God sent His Son to die so that people like me—and you—could live forever with Him in heaven. Yeshua's death flooded the whole world with life—and the best is yet to come. In fact, I am convinced it is just around the corner.

A MAN NAMED LAZARUS

During His time on Earth, Yeshua raised at least three people back to life after they had died. The story of Jairus's daughter is found in the fifth chapter of Mark and the eighth chapter of Luke. His raising to life the son of a widow from the town of Nain is recorded in the seventh chapter of Luke. And in the eleventh chapter of the Gospel of John, we read how Yeshua raised one of His best friends, Lazarus, the brother of Mary and Martha.

It's interesting to me that we know more about Mary and Martha than we do about Lazarus. You may remember that Mary had anointed the Lord with perfume and wiped His feet with her hair, and Martha had complained because—in her opinion—Mary wasn't doing enough to help her provide for the needs of their guests. All we really know about Lazarus is that he was their brother and that he got sick and died. This says something to me about the high regard Yeshua had for Lazarus's two sisters—and for women in general—but I suppose that's a topic for another occasion.

Back to the subject at hand—do you remember what Jesus did when word came to Him that Lazarus was sick? He didn't do anything. He stayed right where He was instead of rushing off to heal His friend. That's certainly not the sort of behavior one would expect, but John 11:5–6 says, "Now *Yeshua* loved Martha and her sister and Lazarus. However, when He heard that Lazarus was sick, He stayed where He was for two more days."

By the time He decided to go up to Bethany to check on him, Lazarus was already dead. The Scriptures tell us that when He came to Lazarus's tomb, "*Yeshua* wept." (John 11:35) That is the shortest verse in the Bible, but it is also one of most thought provoking. Why did Yeshua cry? Was it because He was sad that Lazarus had died? That seems unlikely because He knew He was about to raise His friend back to life. Was it because Mary and Martha didn't seem to understand that He really was "the way, the truth, and the life" (John 14:6), and that He was perfectly able to raise Lazarus from the dead? Perhaps. Or was it because, as some have suggested, He knew He was about to call Lazarus back from Paradise into a world filled with trouble and pain?

We don't know the answer because the Bible doesn't tell us. But I think it's possible that He was weeping for all of us who are caught in death's grip. His tears very well may have been an indication of how much God hates death and how He wants to set us free from its curse. One thing is certain: He longs for each and every one of us to come out of the shadow of death and into the light of eternal life.

> So *Yeshua*, again deeply troubled within Himself, comes to the tomb. It was a cave, and a stone was lying against it. *Yeshua* says, "Roll away the stone!"
>
> Martha, the dead man's sister, said to Him, "Master, by this time he stinks! He's been dead for four days!"
>
> *Yeshua* says to her, "Didn't I tell you that if you believed, you would see the glory of God?"
>
> So they rolled away the stone. *Yeshua* lifted up His eyes and said, "Father, I thank you that you have heard Me. I knew that You always hear Me; but because of this crowd standing around I said it, so that they may believe that You sent Me."
>
> And when He had said this, He cried out with a loud voice, "Lazarus, come out!" He who had been dead came out, wrapped in burial clothes binding his hands and feet, with a cloth over his face. And *Yeshua* tells them, "Cut him loose, and let him go!"
>
> Therefore Judeans, who had come to Miriam and had seen what *Yeshua* had done, put their trust in Him. But some of them went to the Pharisees and told them what *Yeshua* had done.
>
> —JOHN 11:38–46

Why do you suppose Yeshua delayed going to help when His friend was sick? I think there were two reasons. First, because He knew the magnitude of the impact that would come from Lazarus's resurrection. Many of the people who had come to mourn for Lazarus would come to believe in Him when they saw Him bring

Lazarus back to life. In this way, they would receive life from the dead.

The second reason He delayed coming to help was that He knew that Lazarus himself would become a living testimony to God's love and power. If Lazarus had been healed before he died, it would have caused a temporary stir. But being the man who had been brought back to life after being dead for four days is another thing all together. Don't you imagine people came from all over just to get a glimpse of Lazarus or to hear him tell his story? I would certainly want to hear the testimony of a man who had been brought back to life after being dead for four days!

The twelfth chapter of John reports, "Six days before Passover, *Yeshua* came to Bethany, where Lazarus was, whom *Yeshua* had raised from the dead. So they prepared a dinner there for *Yeshua*. Martha was serving, and Lazarus was one of those reclining at the table with Him.... Now a large crowd of Judeans knew He was there and came, not only for *Yeshua* but also to see Lazarus, whom He had raised from the dead. So the ruling *kohanim* made plans to kill Lazarus also, because on account of him many of the Jewish people were going and putting their trust in *Yeshua*." (John 12:1–2, 9–11).

Yeshua's Death Brought Life

Death and life often go hand-in-hand in God's economy. He hates death, He has always hated death, and He is grieved whenever anyone has to die—*has* being the operative word. I think we tend to blame God for death, as if death is one of His creations, something sinister and terrible that He invented.

But that's not the case. God never intended for man to die. Death, both spiritual and physical, is a consequence of sin. Sin brings death just as surely as two plus two makes four. That is why God had already devised a plan to defeat death and was willing to implement it even though it meant agony and death for His only begotten Son.

When Yeshua said, "Father, into Your hands I entrust My spirit," and breathed His last (Luke 23:46), life flowed out from His atoning death and became available to all. As Jesus said, "I have come that they might have life, and have it abundantly!" (John 10:10).

Scripture tells us that when Yeshua died, the veil in the temple was torn in two (Matt. 27:51). What is the significance of this? Hebrews 9:1–9 explains that the veil in the temple separated the holy of holies from the rest of the temple. The holy of holies was the place where God was fully present, and no one but the high priest was allowed to enter, and even then, only once a year. Isaiah 59 tells us that this signified that man was separated from God by sin.

The tearing of the veil signified that sin had been defeated once and for all and that all men and women were now free to come directly into the presence of God. There was no longer any need for a human priest to serve as an intermediary.

When the Messiah died, it seemed as if death had won its biggest victory. Instead, it had suffered its greatest defeat. The Book of Matthew says, "And the tombs were opened, and many bodies of the *kedoshim* [holy ones] who were sleeping were raised to life. And coming forth out of the tombs after His resurrection, they went into the holy city and appeared to many" (Matt. 27:52–53).

What happened to these people who came out of their graves? Did they go on with their lives, living as they had before death so rudely interrupted them? Or, after showing themselves in Jerusalem, did they simply go back to their tombs and lie down again to wait for the time when all of the dead rise on the Day of Judgment? We don't know the answer to either of those questions because the Bible doesn't tell us what happened. And it's not really important anyway. What is important is that death was overcome that day.

Death Becomes Temporary

God was showing that even death is not final. Yeshua broke the chains and turned death into a temporary problem. Once again, life had come from the dead—but this was just a small foretaste of what is yet to come.

The day is coming when all the graves will be opened and all the dead raised, and I believe there is plenty of evidence that this day is drawing near. In the Book of Revelation, John writes of that future day:

> I saw the dead—the great and the small—standing before the throne. The books were opened, and another book was opened—the Book of Life. And the dead were judged according to what was written in the books, according to their deeds. The sea gave up the dead that were in it, and death and *Sheol* gave up the dead in them. Then they were each judged, each one of them, according to their deeds. Then death and *Sheol* were thrown into the lake of fire. This is the second death—the lake of fire.
>
> —Revelation 20:12–14

We previously talked about the fact that Jewish people are coming to know Yeshua in ever-increasing numbers. As this happens, we are gradually seeing the fulfillment of Romans 11:15—life is starting to come from the dead. It is only a trickle now, but it will eventually become a torrent. This world is troubled by sin and hate. In many places—North Korea, Syria, and Iraq, for instance—the darkness is deep indeed, but the light is shining in the darkness.

Bible teacher and author Derek Prince writes:

> We need to understand that the restoration of Israel is, initially, mainly political; ultimately, it will be very spiritual

> indeed. We see this in Jeremiah, where God says: "I will bring Judah and Israel back from captivity and will rebuild them as they were before. I will cleanse them from all the sin they have committed against me and will forgive all their sins of rebellion against me" (Jeremiah 33:7–8, NIV).
>
> Notice the order. God says first He will bring them back to their land; second, He will rebuild them; and, third, He will cleanse them and forgive them. The spiritual restoration is the climax. It is the ultimate objective, but it does not come first. At present, we are seeing the first part of that promise fulfilled. The second and third are sure to follow.[6]

I recently read a newspaper report that seemed to indicate that Israel itself is changing its attitude toward Messianic Jews. According to the *Times of Israel*, "Yaakov Ariel, a professor of religious studies at the University of North Carolina, says there are signs that Jewish groups have grown more accepting of Messianic Jews in recent years. Ariel notes that a recent call by a British Reform rabbi to be more accepting of the movement stirred little outcry. The World Congress of Jewish Studies, which takes place every four years in Jerusalem, featured a panel on Messianic Jews this year—something Ariel has been seeking for decades."[7]

In addition, *Israel Today* reports that Be'ad Chaim, a Messianic pro-life and women's health organization, was given a major award by the Israeli Knesset for its "significant contribution to the protection of mothers and children." What began in the 1980s as a small Messianic prayer group that taught in congregations across Israel and passed out fliers against abortion on street corners has grown into a nationally recognized women's health organization. "Today," the paper notes, "the organization is having a significant impact for change in Israeli society as social workers, welfare officials and needy families around the country refer mothers with unborn children and crisis pregnancies to one of Be'ad Chaim's 12 offices."[8]

I just came back from Israel and met with many of the leaders of Messianic ministries Jewish Voice partners with. They told me incredible stories of Orthodox Jews, even rabbis, secretly believing in Yeshua. Others talked about the growing acceptance they are experiencing from government leaders and the general public. There is no doubt the spiritual climate is shifting.

I don't remember hearing reports like this just a few short years ago. And although there is certainly not a mass revival taking place yet in Israel, these reports do reveal that a change is underway in the hearts of the Jewish people—changes that will ultimately lead to Messiah's return to earth and an outpouring of life from the dead. The old Bob Dylan song is true once again, "The times they are a-changin'."

It's Happening With Muslims Too

I am also hearing incredible reports of Muslims being saved. I even know some former Muslim terrorists who have come to faith. Now they love Israel and the Jewish people!

Heidi Baker of Iris Ministries told CBN News that thousands of Muslims are receiving Jesus as Lord. "It's probably the only place in the world where they are coming so quickly," she said. "Many people are having dreams. They see Jesus appear to them. Probably half our pastors were leaders, imams in Moslem mosques. They were leaders in these mosques, now they're pastors."[9]

CBN's Jerusalem bureau chief, Chris Mitchell, also quoted Christine Darg, author of *The Jesus Visions: Signs and Wonders in the Muslim World*. "He [Yeshua] is going into the Muslim world and revealing, particularly, the last 24 hours of His life—how He died on the cross, which Islam does not teach—how He was raised from the dead, which Islam also does not teach—and how He is the Son of God, risen in power."[10]

Nizar Shaheen, host of Light for the Nations, a Christian program seen throughout the Muslim world, told Mitchell, "We receive lots of letters about people who have had dreams about the Lord, visions, even miracles. When they watch the program, they say yes, we had a dream or a vision, and they accept Jesus as Lord."[11]

One of those who surrendered his life to Yeshua is Samer Achmad Muhammed. He says he hated Christians, but that changed when he heard the gospel. "I dedicated my life to Jesus Christ, Jesus forgave me for my sins," he said. "He gave me eternal life and peace. And the second thing, I really suffered in my daily life, but I had peace, I had joy because Jesus entered my heart."[12]

This is happening more frequently in territories controlled by Islamic State terrorists. As you know, the Islamic State has executed thousands of people in the Middle East, many by beheading and some by crucifixion. It is hard for me to imagine such disregard for human life and lack of compassion for those in pain. And what makes it even more bizarre is that many of those who have been tortured are Muslims—but Muslims who have some doctrinal disagreements with the ISIS murderers. It is these terrorized families who report encounters with Yeshua. He is coming to them out of the darkness and terror, bringing them life from the dead, even though they have never heard His name or called on Him to save them. It is always in the darkness that His light shines the brightest.

In the middle of the darkness that has much of the Middle East in its grip, Christianity.com reports that stories of Muslims coming to faith are cropping up from around the globe. Veteran missionary David Garrison told *World* magazine that "there is a revival in the Muslim world." The author of *A Wind in the House of Islam*, Garrison estimates that between two million and seven million former Muslims have converted to Christianity in the past two decades.[13]

The Light Is Growing in the Midst of the Darkness

The apostle John described Yeshua as the light of the world: "In the beginning was the Word. The Word was with God, and the Word was God. He was with God in the beginning. All things were made through Him, and apart from Him nothing was made that has come into being. In Him was life, and the life was the light of men. The light shines in the darkness, and the darkness has not overpowered it....The true light, coming into the world, gives light to every man" (John 1:1–5, 9).

Many years ago, Knott's Berry Farm, an amusement park in California, had a small chapel that was rented out for weddings and other occasions. The little chapel was replaced long ago by roller coasters and other more "exciting" rides. But back in the day when it was still one of the park's most popular attractions, everyone who came to the chapel received a portrait of Jesus in a prayerful pose. He was dressed in a white robe, His eyes closed in prayer.

But if you held that portrait up to the light for a few moments and then took it into a closet or other dark space, something really cool happened. The robe began to glow a dazzling white, and as you continued to watch, Yeshua's eyelids opened, revealing piercing eyes that seemed to bore right into your soul. The picture was touching and compelling no matter where you looked at it. But viewed in the dark, it was truly amazing.

What does this have to do with the prophetic mysteries of Israel and the end times? Simply this. The world in which we're living is growing darker and darker, but in the midst of that darkness, the light of Yeshua is shining brighter and brighter. As the darkness closes in on us, His brightness will become even more dazzling. The stage for His return is being set, and we have been called to play a part in it. But we have to get off the sidelines and into the game. Like the wise sons of Issachar in 1 Chronicles 12:33, we have to "know how to interpret the signs of the times."

I Would Give Up My Own Salvation

In the last chapter we looked at Romans 9:1–4, where the apostle Paul shares his willingness to give up his own salvation for his unbelieving Jewish brothers, saying: "For I would pray that I myself were cursed, banished from Messiah for the sake of my people—my own flesh and blood, who are Israelites" (Rom. 9:3–4) I shared why I thought this statement was of such great import and the reasons he was willing to go to such great lengths for Israel's salvation. I don't know about you, but I can't think of anything more drastic or precious than to offer one's place in eternity for another. Yet Paul was willing to make this sacrifice.

I want to offer now one final reason: Paul understood that the ultimate result of Israel's acceptance of their Messiah would bring "life from the dead" to the world and the return of Yeshua to the earth. Another way of saying it might be, "For I would be willing to give up my own salvation to see God's ultimate plan for the world accomplished." You see, Paul understood the key to God's plan for the redemption of the world, or "life from the dead," was connected to Israel's salvation, and for that cause Paul was willing to sacrifice his own salvation.

What about you? Are you willing to make the sacrifices necessary to be part of what I believe will be the greatest move of God in history?

Chapter 7

KEY SEVEN: THE RESTORATION OF ALL THINGS

Heaven must receive Him, until the time of the restoration of all the things that God spoke about long ago through the mouth of His holy prophets.

—Acts 3:21

Just before I sat down to write this chapter, I happened to see a news story on TV about another wildfire that was raging through the foothills of Southern California. A reporter was talking to a couple who had lost their home to the fire.

As you might expect, the man and his wife were devastated. They had lived in that house for more than twenty years. Many of their memories were tied up in that house. Their children had grown up there. And now it was gone—forever. My heart went out to that heartbroken couple and to the many others in their neighborhood who had suffered the same sort of loss.

Maybe you have never lost a home to fire, flood, or another disaster, but I know you've suffered devastating loss just the same. Tragically, ever since Adam and Eve sinned in the Garden of Eden, loss is a part of life. People we love die. Possessions that have great value to us are stolen or destroyed. We lose friendships when people move away or grow distant for some reason. Friends we love and trust betray us. Loved ones die of cancer. I know a man who recently lost his job as a teacher because he contracted a disease of the vocal cords that left him unable to speak. His doctors are hoping his speech will return, but they give no guarantees.

Loss is all around us—but it won't always be this way. When the Messianic age comes, God is going to restore to us everything we have lost. And I believe those days of restoration are so near that we can almost reach out and touch them.

I get excited when I read scriptures like the following, from the pen of the apostle Paul:

> I consider the sufferings of this present time not worthy to be compared with the coming glory to be revealed to us. For the creation eagerly awaits the revelation of the sons of God. For the creation was subjected to futility—not willingly but because of the One who subjected it—in hope that the creation itself also will be set free from bondage to decay into the glorious freedom of the children of God. For we know that the whole creation groans together and suffers birth pains until now—and not only creation, but even ourselves. We ourselves, who have the firstfruits of the *Ruach*, groan inwardly as we eagerly wait for adoption—the redemption of our body.
>
> —ROMANS 8:18–23

The prophet Isaiah gives two inspiring prophecies about what this earth will be like when everything is restored to the way it was always meant to be. The first of these is found in the eleventh chapter:

> The wolf will live with the lamb, the leopard will lie down with the goat, the calf and the lion and the yearling together; and a little child will lead them. The cow will feed with the bear, their young will lie down together, and the lion will eat straw like the ox. The infant will play near the cobra's den, and the young child will put its hand into the viper's nest. They will neither harm nor destroy on all my holy mountain, for the earth will be filled with the knowledge of the LORD as the waters cover the sea. In that day the Root of Jesse will stand as a banner for the peoples; the nations will rally to him, and his resting place will be glorious.
>
> —ISAIAH 11:6–10, NIV

This is a great picture of the world the way God meant it to be.

When the "restoration of all things" takes place, the world and everything in it will change for the better. I believe weeds and thistles will be transformed into beautiful flowers and plants. Vicious wild animals will become tame and friendly. Annoying insects will no longer be buzzing around. No child will be hungry, sick, or alone. In fact, no one will be without nutritious food, robust health, or friendship. Starvation and pollution will cease. Best of all, we will all know fellowship with God similar to the fellowship Adam and Eve had with Him in the garden. God Himself says that during those days, "It will come to pass that before they call, I will answer, and while they are still speaking, I will hear" (Isa. 65:24).

First Corinthians 13 speaks of this time when it says, "For now we see in a mirror dimly, but then face to face. Now I know in part, but then I will know fully, even as I have been fully known" (v. 12).

Then refers to the time after the "restoration of all things" has taken place.

The prophet Ezekiel paints a glorious picture of the earth in that day:

> On the day I cleanse you from all your sins, I will resettle your towns, and the ruins will be rebuilt. The desolate land will be cultivated instead of lying desolate in the sight of all who pass through it. They will say, "This land that was laid waste has become like the garden of Eden; the cities that were lying in ruins, desolate and destroyed, are now fortified and inhabited."
>
> —EZEKIEL 36:33–35, NIV

THE JEWISH SAGES WROTE ABOUT IT

The Jewish rabbis of old always believed in and taught about the coming Messianic age, although it is a concept that has been lost to much of Judaism today. I'm often asked what Jews believe about the Messiah and a Messianic age to come. Well, there is no single answer. As we like to joke, when you have two Jews, you end up with three opinions. I would say that a majority of the Jewish community has become increasingly secularized over the last century, and many no longer believe literally in a coming Messiah. They have relegated the Messianic age to an idealist, utopian era that will be brought about by acts of benevolence and social justice. You can see this thinking manifest in the activities and viewpoints of the left-leaning Jewish community today.

It is the observant Orthodox Jewish minority that still hold to a literal interpretation of Scripture, including the coming of the Messiah and the establishment of a literal Messianic age expected by their earlier sages. The influential Rabbi Maimonides wrote:

> The Messianic age is when the Jews will regain their independence and all return to the land of Israel. The Messiah will be a very great king, he will achieve great fame, and his reputation among the gentile nations will be even greater than that of King Solomon. His great righteousness and the wonders that he will bring about will cause all peoples to make peace with him and all lands to serve him.... Nothing will change in the Messianic age, however, except that Jews will regain their independence.... Rich and poor, strong and weak, will still exist. However it will be very easy for people to make a living, and with very little effort they will be able to accomplish very much.... War shall not exist, and nation shall no longer lift up sword against nation.... The Messianic age will be highlighted by a community of the righteous and dominated by goodness and wisdom. It will be ruled by the Messiah, a righteous and honest king, outstanding in wisdom, and close to God....Our sages and prophets did not long for the Messianic age in order that they might rule the world and dominate the gentiles, the only thing they wanted was to be free for Jews to involve themselves with the Torah and its wisdom.[1]

There are other teachings about the end of days in the Talmud, such as this passage from the tractate Sanhedrin, which speaks of the Messiah's coming:

> R. Johanan said: When you see a generation ever dwindling, hope for him [the Messiah], as it is written, And the afflicted people thou wilt save.
>
> R. Johanan said: When thou seest a generation overwhelmed by many troubles as by a river, await him, as it is written, when the enemy shall come in like a flood, the Spirit of the Lord shall lift up a standard against him; which is followed by, And the Redeemer shall come to Zion.

> R. Johanan also said: The son of David will come only in a generation that is either altogether righteous or altogether wicked, "in a generation that is altogether righteous,"—as it is written, Thy people also shall be all righteous: they shall inherit the land for ever. "Or altogether wicked,"—as it is written, And he saw that there was no man, and wondered that there was no intercessor; and it is [elsewhere] written, For mine own sake, even for mine own sake, will I do it.[2]

A Transformation Is on the Way

This world is like a butterfly about to emerge from a dark and lifeless-looking cocoon.

I believe the transformation of a lowly caterpillar into a gorgeous butterfly is one of God's most striking miracles. A little wormlike creature wraps itself into a cloak made of threads from its own body. For the next week or ten days, it stays inside that little brown or gray sack that looks like a leaf or a small twig. There's nothing to call attention to it. It seems dull and lifeless, but if we could see what was happening inside that cocoon, we'd be amazed. The caterpillar is actually disintegrating, digesting itself and completely rearranging its body. Colorful wings are growing. Eyes are developing. Six long legs are taking shape.

Soon the newly formed butterfly will begin to emerge. It bears no resemblance to the ugly caterpillar. The insect's wings are covered with intricate patterns—circles, swirls, stripes, and other designs made up of dazzling colors. The dull caterpillar that once spent its days crawling in the dirt is now a beautiful butterfly floating on the breeze.

This world has been wrapped in the cocoon of sin and disobedience for far too long. Any day now, an unbelievable transformation will take place. It will be thrilling, exhilarating, glorious, and the beginning of a beautiful eternity for those who love the Lord and have accepted the salvation He offers.

C. S. Lewis didn't talk much about butterflies, but he expressed a similar thought: "This world is a great sculptor's shop. We are the statues and there's a rumor going around the shop that some of us are someday going to come to life."[3]

The Connection Between Israel and the Church

I believe this "coming to life" is directly tied in to what is going on in Israel today and among Jewish people around the world. I'm convinced that there is a direct correlation between the health of Israel and the health of the church. There have been many times when a blessing upon Israel has led to a corresponding revival in the church. Here are some examples:

The birth of the Zionist movement and the Azusa Street Revival

In chapter 4, I introduced Theodor Herzl and talked about the birth of the Zionist movement. What I want you to be aware of now is that as this movement for a Jewish state in the Middle East began to gather momentum in Europe and North America, parallel to this a revival broke out the United States. Known as the Pentecostal revival, it first emerged in Zion, Illinois, a small city founded by a Scottish evangelist and faith healer named John Alexander Dowie in 1900, just three years after the World Zionist Congress first convened. Dowie was a forerunner of Pentecostalism and saw a major outbreak of the *charismata* (gifts of the Spirit) in his meetings—phenomena such as divine healing, miracles, and glossolalia (speaking in unknown tongues).

A better known revival broke out a few years later in 1906 in Los Angeles. Led by William J. Seymour, an African American preacher, the Azusa Street Revival started with a worship service on April 9, 1906, and continued every night for about ten years. The revival was characterized by speaking in tongues, visions, dramatic salvations and healings, and other evidences of the Holy Spirit.

The rebirth of Israel and the Latter Rain movement

In 1948 the State of Israel was reestablished as the homeland for the Jewish people. Again, revival broke out in the church, this time in the form of the "Latter Rain" movement, which began just a few months after Israel became a state. It originated at Sharon Bible College, a first-year school in Saskatchewan in Canada. On Easter weekend in 1948, a "Feast of Pentecost" service was held at the school. The original service lasted for days and was the catalyst for the first camp meeting held July 7–18, 1948, which drew thousands of people to the college. The Latter Rain revival—which was marked by speaking in tongues, prophecy, and miracles—quickly spread throughout Canada, the United States, and around the world.

The Six-Day War, Jerusalem's restoration, and the Jesus movement

In 1967 war broke out again in Israel. I spoke about the miraculous victory that took place in what became known as the Six-Day War. For six days the war raged, and on the seventh day they rested. Talk about the hand of God being visible!

As a result of this short war, Israel took control of the Gaza Strip, the Sinai Peninsula, the West Bank, and the Golan Heights. Most important, the Old City of Jerusalem, including the Temple Mount and ancient Jewish Quarter, came back under Jewish control.

Just a short time later, a revival known by some as the "Jesus movement" ignited in California and quickly spread throughout the United States and around the world. Thousands of college students and other young people discovered the love and power of

God. Wikipedia says, "Although the Jesus movement lasted no more than a decade (except for the Jesus People USA which continues to exist in Chicago), its influence on Christian culture can still be seen. Thousands of converts moved into leadership positions in churches and parachurch organizations. The informality of the Jesus movement's music and worship affected almost all evangelical churches. Some of the fastest growing US denominations of the late 20th century, such as Calvary Chapel, Hope Chapel Churches, and the Vineyard Churches, trace their roots directly back to the Jesus movement...Perhaps the most significant and lasting influence, however, was the growth of an emerging strand within evangelical Christianity that appealed to the contemporary youth culture."[4] Although the Jesus movement lasted only about ten years, it had a profound influence on the church. Most of the current leadership of the Messianic Jewish movement and many prominent pastors of large, charismatic churches came out of this move of God.

The Russian aliyah and the Toronto Blessing

During the 1990s an estimated one million Jews flooded out of the former Soviet Union to begin new lives in Israel. This was a direct fulfillment of Jeremiah 16:14–15:

> "Therefore, the days are quickly coming," declares *Adonai*, "when it will no longer be said. 'As *Adonai* lives, who brought up the children of Israel out of the land of Egypt.' Rather, 'As *Adonai* lives, who brought up the children of Israel from the land of the north and from all the lands where He had banished them.' So I will bring them back into their land that I gave to their fathers."

Note that this prophecy mentions this return will begin from the north. God wasn't talking about North America; He was referring to the land north of Israel. Guess where you end up if you draw a straight line north of Jerusalem? The answer is Russia.

The Russian exodus began with the fall of the Iron Curtain at the end of the 1980s. Over a fifteen-year period, over one million Russian-speaking Jews left the oppression of the former Soviet Empire and moved to Israel. It was the largest aliyah in the seventy-year history of that tiny nation.

As this prophetic aliyah from the north was taking place, a powerful revival known as the Toronto Blessing emerged. It started with 120 people meeting in a small church near Toronto's Pearson International Airport. Before the revival drew to a close several years later, hundreds of thousands of people in Toronto and other cities around the world had been impacted.

One of the hallmarks of the Toronto Blessing was something that became known as "holy laughter," an outpouring of the Holy Spirit that caused people to laugh hilariously. In some cases, thousands of people were hit by holy laughter at the same time. They laughed until tears rolled down their cheeks. Sometimes they laughed so hard and long that they could no longer stand or sit, falling onto the floor where they lay helplessly, continuing to laugh as if they had just heard the funniest joke of all time. Soon, holy laughter was occurring in Pentecostal and Charismatic churches around the world. I personally experienced this outbreak during meetings in our Bible school between 1994 and 1996 while I was living in St. Petersburg, Russia.

I am convinced there is a pattern here, a link between this massive return of the Jewish people to their land from the north and the outpouring of blessing upon the church. I don't think it is just a coincidence that the Toronto outpouring was characterized by holy laughter and joy and Psalm 126:1–3 (NIV) describes the return of Israel to their land in this way:

> When the LORD restored the fortunes of Zion, we were like those who dreamed. Our mouths were filled with laughter, our tongues with songs of joy. Then it was said among the nations, "The LORD has done great things for them." The LORD has done great things for us, and we are filled with joy.

What Is the Fullness of the Gentiles?

Previously, we discussed the fact that Yeshua said Jerusalem would be trampled underfoot by the Gentiles until the times of the Gentiles are fulfilled (Luke 21:24). In our day, we are seeing this prophecy coming to pass. As I write these words, the United States is considering moving its embassy from Tel Aviv to Jerusalem. This would be a significant step toward recognizing that Jerusalem is the true capital of Israel, and it would result in great blessing for the United States. Tel Aviv is a wonderful city, the first modern Jewish city in the Middle East, having been established in 1909.[5] But it is not the city where the great king David ruled and to which the Messiah will return. That honor goes to Jerusalem.

We have also been witnessing the blindness gradually coming off the eyes of the Jewish people in greater and greater numbers as Paul wrote in the eleventh chapter of Romans, that "a partial hardening [or blindness] has come upon Israel until the fullness of the Gentiles has come in" (Rom. 11:25). I told you that many people interpret the word *fullness* as "full number"—as if some specific number of Gentiles must be saved before the eyes of the Jewish people will be opened and they will come to the Messiah in great numbers. But as I stated before, I don't see it this way. I believe Romans 11:25 means that in addition to the "fullness of time" I already spoke of, this refers to the church coming into the fullness of her identity. The church must claim its full heritage as children of Abraham, who as wild olive branches have been grafted into the natural olive tree, which is Israel. (See Romans 11:17.) After a seventeen-hundred-year separation, the church needs to return to the Jewish roots of her faith and thus experience the fullness of her identity.

Does this mean Gentile believers must observe all the Jewish feast days, hold services on Saturdays, and learn to speak Hebrew? Of course not. But it does mean Gentile believers should strive to understand the Jewish origins of their faith and do what they can to build bridges of understanding and fellowship with their Jewish friends, neighbors, and coworkers. After all, Jesus was born to Jewish parents in the Jewish homeland of Israel. He grew up as other Jewish children did. He went to the temple, and He and His family always observed the *moed'im*, the appointed feasts and festivals of the *Torah*. All of His disciples were Jews, and He said He came to reach the lost sheep of Israel. Christians must help their Jewish friends understand that Jesus, the Savior they love, is the Jewish Messiah Yeshua, that the God they serve is the God of Abraham, Isaac, and Jacob. The God of Israel. They must help them overcome the erroneous view many Jews have that Christians believe in a different God and a different Bible.

I don't want you to misunderstand what I am saying here. Yeshua came to die for everyone. The Scriptures are very clear about that. But while He was present on Earth in a human body, Jesus's ministry was directed to the Jews.

I have to admit that it bothers me when I meet Christians who have no interest at all in the Old Testament and don't appreciate the Jewish origins of their faith. As I've already stated, the promise of the new covenant was given to the Jew first and then to the Gentiles. It is only through faith in Israel's Messiah, Yeshua, that Gentiles are able to experience all the blessings given first to the descendants of Abraham.

I know some Jewish believers in Jesus who good-naturedly refer to themselves as "completed" or "fulfilled" Jews. This means they enjoy the full blessings of both their Jewish heritage and their new covenant faith in Messiah. They are blessed to be children of Abraham both by birth and through acceptance of the Messiah who came through him. The same is true of those of us who call ourselves Messianic Jews. We remain Jews by heritage but also are Messianic because of our faith in Israel's Messiah.

Far too many Gentile Christians are missing the blessings that could be theirs if they would fully embrace their Hebraic heritage. One of those blessings is playing a role in removing the blindness from the eyes of the Jewish people as they witness the fullness of the church's Jewish identity being restored.

Yeshua Is Waiting in Heaven to Return

As an evangelist myself, I love the story of Peter and John healing the lame man as they were entering the temple to worship. This miracle created a great stir among the people, and a great crowd formed as a result. I love miracles because they create opportunities to share my faith with others. That is exactly what happens in this story, recorded for us in Acts chapter 3. Peter seizes the opportunity and begins to proclaim the gospel to the crowd:

> While he was clinging to Peter and John, all the people together came running toward them in the place called Solomon's Portico. But when Peter saw, he responded to the people, "Men of Israel, why are you amazed at this? Why do you stare at us—as if by our own power or godliness we had made this man walk? The God of Abraham and Isaac and Jacob, the God of our fathers, has glorified His Servant *Yeshua*—the One you handed over and disowned before

> Pilate, though he had decided to release Him. But you rejected the Holy and Righteous One and asked for a murderer to be granted to you. You killed the Author of life—the One God raised from the dead! We are witnesses of it. Now through faith in the name of *Yeshua*, His name has strengthened this man whom you see and know. Indeed, the faith through *Yeshua* has given this man perfect health in front of you all. Now brothers, I know that you acted in ignorance, just as your leaders did. But what God foretold through the mouth of all His prophets—that His Messiah was to suffer—so He has fulfilled."
>
> —ACTS 3:11–18

What a powerful message. And then he follows with the altar call:

> Repent, therefore, and return—so your sins might be blotted out, so times of relief might come from the presence of *ADONAI* and He might send *Yeshua*, the Messiah appointed for you. Heaven must receive Him, until the time of the restoration of all the things that God spoke about long ago through the mouth of His holy prophets.
>
> —ACTS 3:19–21

Now let's look carefully at this passage. I see a progression here. First, Peter is imploring his Jewish brethren to repent and return to God. The Hebrew word *t'shuva* is often translated "convert," but it literally means to "turn around." We were walking in the wrong direction, away from God. Now we must make a 180-degree turn to face God. When we do this, our sins are forgiven and we are saved.

Peter is first referring to the Jewish people alone. If they repent and turn around, their sins will be forgiven and blotted out. But then he expands his statement beyond them. In other words, he is telling the Jewish people, "If you repent, your sins will be forgiven and as a result, times of relief from the presence of the Lord will be poured out upon all."

Other translations say "times of refreshing" instead of "times of relief." I believe the verse is talking about an outpouring of revival upon the nations when the people of Israel repent and turn to their Messiah. In fact, many revivalists point to Acts 3:20—times of refreshing from the presence of the Lord—as the classic definition of revival.

But it doesn't stop there. Peter goes on to say as a result of their return to God, not only will He send revival, but He will also send Yeshua. Peter is saying the same thing Paul said in Romans 11:26—that Jesus can only return when the Jewish people receive their Messiah.

But until that set time occurs, Yeshua is waiting in heaven to return.

The Restoration the Prophets Spoke Of

Let's now look a bit closer at this statement Peter makes in Acts 3:21—"until the time of the restoration of all the things that God spoke about long ago through the mouth of His holy prophets," or as the NIV says, "until the time comes for God to restore everything, as he promised long ago through his holy prophets." What is the restoration promised through the prophets he is speaking about? We need to understand this because until we see these things come to pass, Yeshua cannot return.

I believe much of this promised restoration has already been fulfilled. The rebirth of Israel and the reestablishment of Jerusalem are both part of the promised regathering or physical restoration of the Jewish people back to their land. The migrations back to the land such as the Russian-speaking Jewish community returning to Israel from the north (now numbering over one million)[6] and the Ethiopian Jews from the south (over 140,000) are part of this.[7] This is a direct fulfillment of Isaiah 11:11, Jeremiah 16:14–16, and numerous other prophecies found in the Old Testament concerning the return of the children of Israel to their ancient land.

We are also witnessing a growing number of Jewish people who are recognizing Jesus as their Messiah. The birth of the modern Messianic Jewish movement after the restoration of Jerusalem in 1967 and the rapid expansion of this movement around the world are also signs of the restoration of all things Peter was speaking of. This restoration includes both the Jews' physical restoration back to the land and spiritual restoration back to their God through the one name given under heaven through which we must be saved, Jesus of Nazareth. What now remains for this restoration to be complete is the fulfillment of Romans 11:26—"and so all Israel will be saved" (NKJV).

Peter's declaration in Acts 3 directly ties Israel's repentance and acceptance of its Messiah to times of refreshing, which I see as revival, coming to the nations. This will culminate in the return of Yeshua, who will reign from Jerusalem, put an end to sickness and death, and restore the earth to its state before Adam and Eve sinned.

Tough Times Are Ahead

I now need to address an area I frankly don't enjoy talking about—persecution and tribulation in the days ahead. Another thing both the prophets and apostles told us is that a time of great tribulation would come upon the earth in the end of the age immediately preceeding the Messiah's return. In fact, this period of great turmoil on the earth is a necessary part of the process of bringing about the "restoration of all things." This tribulation and turmoil are the result of three things:

1. The growing sin and evil throughout the earth

In Matthew 24, Yeshua answers a question from His disciples: "Tell us, when will these things happen? What will be the sign of Your coming and of the end of the age?" (v. 3).

He responds with a rather thorough list of signs. He describes a world filled with turmoil and corrupted by sin, evil, and deception. And perhaps even more frightening is the condition of those who once loved the Lord: "And then many will fall away and will betray one another and hate one other. Many false prophets will arise and lead many astray. Because lawlessness will multiply, the love of many will grow cold" (Matt. 24:10–12).

Yeshua also gives us another clue about the end of the age when He says, "For just as the days of Noah were, so will be the coming of the Son of Man" (Matt. 24:37). Think of what happened in the days of Noah. The world had grown so evil that God decided to use a universal flood to wipe away a corrupt, polluted world and start over. I think the single saddest passage in the entire Bible is Genesis 6:5–6: "Then *Adonai* saw that the wickedness of humankind was great on the earth, and that every inclination of the thoughts of their heart was only evil all the time. So *Adonai* regretted that He made humankind on the earth, and His heart was deeply pained."

Yeshua connected the time before His return with the days of Noah. People were eating, drinking, and celebrating, unaware of how decadent and evil their society had become and unaware of what was about to befall them. Sounds like today, doesn't it?

Noah and his family were saved because of Noah's righteousness. While he and his family were building the ark, the door was open. Others could have repented of their sins, come to God, and been spared from the cataclysm that was about to come on the earth.

But no one would do it. The Bible does not say this, but I wonder if some people were trying to straddle the fence, thinking, "This old Noah seems like a bit of a kook, but who knows? I'll wait and see. If it turns out that he's actually right, I'm sure he'll let me into the ark."

But when the rain began to pour down, the Bible says God closed the door of the ark (Gen. 7:16). Noah didn't do it; God did. I believe that once He had shut that door, no one else could open it.

I'm not trying to scare anyone. The fact that a time of restoration and recovery is coming should be very good news for us all. But we must be ready, and that means living each day like tomorrow is the last. This makes me think of the parable of the ten virgins in Matthew 25.

Ten virgins went out to meet the bridegroom, but five were wise and five were foolish. The foolish virgins took their lamps but had no oil. The wise had extra oil with them in case they needed it. The bridegroom took a long time coming, and it was the middle of the night when someone shouted that he was near. The virgins got up to go meet him, but only five virgins had oil for their lamps. The foolish virgins asked the wise young women to share, but they couldn't. "No, there won't be enough for us and for you" (Matt. 25:9). So they told them to go buy some for themselves.

The bridegroom came while the foolish virgins were off buying oil. "And those who were ready went in with him to the wedding feast, and the door was shut. Now later, the other virgins came, saying, 'Sir, Sir, open up for us!' But he replied, 'Amen, I tell you, I do not know you.' Therefore stay alert, for you know neither the day nor the hour" (Matt. 25:10–13).

If you need to get your relationship with God in order, do it! If you have not accepted Yeshua as your Lord and Savior yet, please do it now. Time may be running out. There is nothing to be gained by delaying—but so much to be lost. The Bible tells us God is not willing that any should perish (2 Pet. 3:9). Don't be like the foolish virgins. Be ready!

2. An increase in demonic activity and intensity

The devil knows exactly what season we are in. He is like a wounded animal lashing out to inflict as much damage as possible because he understands that time is running out. He knows he's doomed, but he's not going to go quietly. Much of his fury is aimed at the Jews since they are at the center of God's end-time plan.

The increase of anti-Semitism around the world is a sure sign that the end is drawing near. According to CNN:

> In the first three months of this year, the number of anti-Semitic incidents in the U.S. was 86 percent higher than the same period last year, says a new report.
>
> The report, released...by the Anti-Defamation League, counted 541 anti-Semitic attacks and threats between January and March.
>
> There were 281 incidents in the same time period in 2016.
>
> Overall, the picture was pretty grim last year too. The ADL says anti-Semitic [incidents] were up by more than a third last year, compared with 2015.[8]

And although he sees some reasons for optimism, ADL's executive director, Abraham Foxman, acknowledged in the *Huffington Post* that "the anti-Semitism news from Europe in over the past year has been terrible: Jews murdered in Paris and Copenhagen, synagogues attacked by mobs and firebombed, and increasing Jewish emigration attributed to fear of more attacks."[9]

Satan is on the attack. But that's good news because it means our Messiah will soon return!

Sometimes Satan will try to deceive us by presenting himself as an angel of light. Paul writes, "The coming of the lawless one is connected to the activity of satan, with all power and signs and false wonders, and with every kind of wicked deception toward those who are perishing" (2 Thess. 2:9–10). It's hard for me to imagine that millions of people all over the world will take the devil's side in the final battle for control of the universe, but I know it's true. They simply can't accept the fact that Yeshua is exactly who He said He is, the King of kings and Lord of lords. They cannot see the truth, and so they fall for a vicious lie.

There are others who won't fall for the devil's lies, and he will do everything he can to destroy them. The apostle Peter puts it this way: "Stay alert! Watch out! Your adversary the devil prowls around like a roaring lion, searching for someone to devour. Stand up against him, firm in your faith, knowing that the same kinds of suffering are being laid upon your brothers and sisters throughout the world" (1 Pet. 5:8–9). Then he delivers this promise, "After you have suffered a little while, the God of all grace—who has called you into His eternal glory in Messiah—will Himself restore, support, strengthen, and establish you" (1 Pet. 5:10). The devil knows exactly what season we are in. He is like a wounded animal, and he is taking his final stand.

3. The judgment of God upon the earth

This is a difficult subject because the God I know is merciful and kind. He is patient and loving and doesn't want anyone to suffer. When we do suffer, He empathizes with us. Because the Lord lived in human form and suffered for us, He knows what it's like to endure physical and emotional pain. And yet despite God's loving nature, the Bible teaches that when we wander away from Him, He sometimes allows us to suffer. He does this hoping it will make us realize how much we need Him and seek to restore our relationship with Him.

Yom Teruah, the Feast of Trumpets (Lev. 23:24), prophetically points to the blowing of the trumpets in heaven to release judgments upon the earth. Prayerfully read Revelation chapters 8 and 9 to get a full picture of the devastation these divine judgements unleash upon the earth. I see these judgments in the light of God's love, His final attempt to get people to turn back to Him. Look around and you will see that it's already happening.

We can see God's judgment in the AIDS epidemic that struck the world beginning in 1981 and has killed over 35 million people to date.[10] The outbreak of violence all around us is another sign of judgment—the mass shootings and other unfathomable criminal acts that seem to happen almost every week. Another is the unbelievable depravity of ISIS and other Islamist extremist groups who torture and slaughter innocent families and children.

The list goes on and on. I want to be clear—I am not saying God is causing any of these things. I believe they are happening because our first ancestors brought sin and thus death upon mankind, and it has corrupted and weakened our planet. But God is using them to eradicate all evil from the universe once and for all.

And if you belong to God, you have absolutely nothing to worry about. If you have accepted Yeshua as your Lord and Savior and are living for Him, you can be sure that He is watching over and protecting you. In the midst of all the distressing, frightening things that are going on in the world today, we can say with the psalmist, "My God is my rock, in Him I take refuge, my shield, my horn of salvation, my stronghold" (Ps. 18:3). We can also trust Yeshua's word when He said, "I am the resurrection and the life! Whoever believes in Me, even if he dies, shall live. And whoever lives and believes in Me shall never die" (John 11:25–26).

These, then, are the three reasons there is such tribulation and turmoil in these last days:

- sin and evil are growing throughout the earth;
- there is an increase of demonic activity;
- God's judgment is being poured out on the earth.

All Curses Will Be Removed

When Adam and Eve sinned in the Garden of Eden, they—and all humankind—were placed under a curse. God told Adam that he would struggle against thorns and thistles to grow enough food for his family. He told Eve that she would suffer the pain of childbirth. Every tear, every pain, every broken heart—all of these things came as a result of the curse. But when the Messiah returns, the curse will be lifted—forever.

Revelation 22:3 promises, "There shall be no more curse, but the throne of God and of the Lamb shall be in it, and His servants shall serve Him" (NKJV). Because there will be no more sin, "there shall be no more death, nor sorrow, nor crying. There shall be no more pain, for the former things [will] have passed away" (Rev. 21:4, NKJV).

Until then, everywhere we look in this world, we will see the results of the curse brought upon us by sin. We see it in disease, violence, and natural disasters. It is truly heartbreaking. Just this year, I lost my brother Dave to bone marrow cancer. His fight had been long and very difficult. I loved him dearly, and seeing what he went through was heartbreaking for me. I'm still grieving this loss.

Why did he have to suffer? Why did he die so young? He was just fifty-eight years old. It was because of the curse. If this world wasn't under a curse, there would be no such thing as cancer. But the day is coming soon when the curse will be lifted and cancer will disappear forever. So will heart disease, AIDS, multiple sclerosis, and every other painful and potentially deadly disease you can think of.

Not long ago, we heard the heartbreaking news that a young boy, only six years old, had died from injuries suffered in yet another school shooting.[11] Why did this child, full of life and potential, die in the very dawn of his life? Why were his parents' hearts shattered in such a way? And why have we been rocked by so many school shootings over the past few years? Again, the answer is that these tragedies happen because of the curse. I long for the day when the curse will be lifted and there will be no more senseless tragedies, and every child will be safe and secure. There will be no more child abuse, childhood diseases, bullies, or anything else to bring tears to the eyes of children and their parents.

Two other tragedies unfolded as I wrote this chapter. First, a category 4 hurricane roared through the Caribbean and headed for the East Coast of the United States. Hundreds of people died in Haiti, and more than a million Floridians were ordered to evacuate their homes on the Atlantic Coast.[12] Then, as I was working on the final edit, another massive hurricane ripped through Texas and Louisiana, causing billions of dollars in damage and leaving thousands homeless. It was the worst hurricane in American history and will take years to rebuild all that was lost.[13] Why does our earth so often seem to be at war with itself? Again, the answer is the sin that has corrupted our world and our universe and left us under a curse.

We can rejoice to know that our Messiah's soon return will bring all of this to an end. Very soon there will be no more hurricanes, tornadoes, floods, earthquakes, wildfires, volcanic eruptions, or any other natural disasters that rip communities apart and leave people struggling to survive.

After the resurrection of all who have ever lived, death itself will come to an end (Isa. 25:8; 1 Cor. 15:26, 54). God will dwell in our midst in a way we have never known. As John the Apostle saw in the vision he recorded in the Book of Revelation, "Behold, the tabernacle of God is with men, and He will dwell with them, and they shall be His people. God Himself will be with them and be their God" (Rev. 21:3, NKJV).

BEAUTY BENEATH THE GRIME

Do you ever watch the television program *Pawn Stars*? I don't see it very often. My schedule is such that I don't have much time for watching TV. Still, I like to sneak a quick peek at it whenever I can. Even if you don't watch it, you've probably heard of it and know how it works, because it's been a staple of the History Channel for a number of years now.

Last year my wife and I visited their shop in Las Vegas with the kids just to see if it looked the same as it did on TV. Scores of people come with their treasures (or junk) to have them appraised and find out if they're really worth anything. It's fun to see someone come in with an item they've had hidden away in the attic and find out it's worth thousands of dollars. It may look like an old piece of junk, but it turns out to be worth a fortune.

I admit that I'm not always the best when it comes to figuring out what the most valuable items are. If you're not an expert, it's hard to tell—especially if something has been in an attic or cellar where it's been gathering dust for years. Sometimes a little sprucing up can turn a piece of junk into a breathtaking masterpiece.

This world we live in is covered with the dust and grime of centuries of sin and disobedience to God. It has been tattered and tarnished almost beyond recognition. Even so, we sometimes see glimpses of what it was meant to be. There are beautiful sunsets and sunrises. Pristine mountain lakes. A rainbow that stretches from one horizon to the other. The beauty and fragrance of a rose. A mother's love and willingness to sacrifice herself for her child. A married couple who truly love each other and who both obey the Bible's command to esteem the other higher than they do themselves. These are all reminders of the way God meant the world to be. But I believe all of these things will be so much more beautiful when the restoration of all things is finally here. As the apostle Paul explained: "For now we see in a mirror dimly, but then face to face. Now I know in part, but then I will know fully, even as I have been fully known" (1 Cor. 13:12).

Not too long ago, I saw a story about a classic painting that was discovered in a corner in an attic, covered by a thick layer of dust. The painting, nearly two hundred years old, was a portrait of a woman named Effie Gray. It was painted by a well-known English artist, John Everett Millais, and was valued at over fifty thousand pounds—or what is now roughly sixty-five thousand American dollars.

The painting was spotted by auctioneer Duncan Chilcott, who had been invited by the property owner to look at a table and some other items that were in the attic. He said, "On the other side of the room behind some old mattresses I saw the painting leaning against the wall. It was covered in thick dust and I was astonished when I blew it off and saw what was beneath."[14]

The forty-five-year-old woman who owned the painting said her mother had given it to her for her ninth birthday. Chilcott said that "judging by the layer of dust on it, it had been in the attic for a very long time, during which it has been lost to the art world."[15]

Even though the world we live in has been tainted by centuries of sin, the original beauty of creation is still there underneath all that mess. It hasn't been lost forever. Someday—and I believe that day will be very soon—all of that dirt will be removed and we will see the world and the universe as God intended it to be! The apostle Paul spoke to this when he wrote, "Things no eye has seen and no ear has heard, that have not entered the heart of mankind—these things God has prepared for those who love Him" (1 Cor. 2:9).

Ten Hallmarks of the Messianic Age

The Scriptures give dozens of examples of the glorious events that will take place during the coming Messianic age. These include:

1. All people everywhere will worship the God of Israel (Isa. 2:1–2).
2. Evil will be defeated (Isa. 11:4).
3. The world will be filled with the knowledge of God (Isa. 11:9).
4. All Israel will know the Lord (Jer. 31:33; Rom. 11:26).
5. The Jewish people with be regathered fully to their homeland (Isa. 11:12; Zech. 10:6).
6. There will be no more death, sorrow, or pain (Isa. 25:8; Rev. 21:4).
7. The dead will rise again (Isa. 26:19).
8. Weapons of war will be destroyed (Ezek. 39:9).
9. The temple will be rebuilt (Ezek. 40).
10. Barren land will become fruitful again (Isa. 51:3; Ezek. 36:29–30; Amos 9:13–15).

Speaking of this time, Yeshua says, "Behold, I am making all things new!...It is done! I am the Alpha and the Omega, the Beginning and the End." (Rev. 21:5–6).

You Have an Important Role to Play

I want you to know that you have an important part to play in these final days of human history. We all do. I'm not exactly sure why this is true. I know that God is all-powerful and that He can do anything He chooses to do any time He chooses to do it. And yet He has chosen us to work with Him as partners in His vineyard. As an example of this, consider prayer. We know that prayer is powerful. As Alfred Lord Tennyson wrote, "More things are wrought by prayer than this world dreams of."[16] I believe it is only because God chose to allow us to partner with Him that prayer is so effective.

Years ago I saw this statement written on a marquee in front of a church, and I thought it was very well said: "Remember, the effectiveness of a prayer doesn't depend upon the one who prays, but rather upon the One who hears." In other words, don't think for a second that there is no power in your prayers because you feel inadequate or unworthy. God is listening, and He will answer.

When I told you that you have an important role to play in this final great move of God and great wrap-up of human history, you may have thought, "Who, me? Are you joking?" Not at all. Before He ascended into heaven, Yeshua Himself told His disciples, "This Good News of the kingdom shall be proclaimed in the whole world as a testimony to all the nations, and then the end will come" (Matt. 24:14).

The way I read this is that the gospel must be preached to every nation on Earth prior to the Messiah's return. Who shares the good news of God's love and supports efforts to spread it into every nation? It's us—you and me! I want to again quote from Romans chapter 10: "How then shall they call on the One in whom they have not trusted? And how shall they trust in the One they have not heard of? And how shall they hear without someone proclaiming?...So faith comes from hearing, and hearing by the word of Messiah" (Rom. 10:14, 17).

People are not going to be saved unless they believe, and for that to happen they first must hear. You have to tell them. One of the most important ways you can be directly involved in Yeshua's return is to spread the good news of eternal life by sharing your faith with those around you. And remember, it's to the Jew first!

Conclusion

FIGHT THE GOOD FIGHT

ARE YOU FAMILIAR with the story of Nehemiah? You can find it in the biblical book that bears his name. Nehemiah was a cup bearer for Artaxerxes, king of Persia, following the Babylonian captivity about 450 years before Yeshua's birth. At this time, Jews were permitted to return to their homeland, but what they found there was a nation in ruins. Nehemiah sought God in prayer, repenting on behalf of those who had turned against Him and disobeyed His laws.

After that, he went to the king and asked for permission to return to Judah and rebuild the city of Jerusalem. Artaxerxes agreed, sending him to Judah as governor of the province, a position Nehemiah held for twelve years. The king furnished Nehemiah with letters explaining his support for the rebuilding of Jerusalem and provided timber from his forests.

The problem for Nehemiah and his workers was that even

though the king supported the project, the Jewish people had many enemies in the land who didn't. And those enemies—Samaritans, Ammonites, Philistines, and Arabs—banded together to fight the restoration of Israel. But Nehemiah waited on God. He depended on God and obeyed the Lord when He spoke. He fought the good fight.

We must be like Nehemiah, walking in obedience day after day, calling on God and asking Him what we can do to help bring about His plans to redeem and restore this world He created. The difference between us and Nehemiah is that he had to fight with physical weapons of war against flesh-and-blood enemies, whereas we are fighting spiritual warfare against Satan and his demons. But the battle is every bit as real and every bit as important as it was for Nehemiah.

Winter Is Almost Over

In his classic book series The Chronicles of Narnia, C. S. Lewis writes of a land where it is always winter but never Christmas. It is a cold, forbidding place ruled by the White Queen, a wicked creature who lives in a frozen palace. Throughout the seven-book series, Lewis tells the adventures of a group of ordinary boys and girls who fight alongside a majestic lion named Aslan to defeat the evil White Queen and restore Narnia to the way it was always intended to be. Although there are many temporary victories along the way, Narnia is finally restored in the last pages of the seventh book of the series, *The Last Battle.*

Though the land looked familiar, there was something different about it. Somehow the "new" Narnia seemed more like the real thing.

Suddenly Farsight the Eagle spread his wings, soared thirty or forty feet up into the air, circled round and then alighted on the ground.

"Kings and Queens," he cried, "we have all been blind. We are only beginning to see where we are... Narnia is not dead. This is Narnia."...

"The Eagle is right," said the Lord Digory.... "The Narnia you were thinking of... was only a shadow or a copy of the real Narnia which has always been here and always will be here: just as our own world, England and all, is only a shadow or copy of something in Aslan's real world. You need not mourn over Narnia, Lucy. All of the old Narnia that mattered, all the dear creatures, have been drawn into the real Narnia through the Door. And of course it is different; as different as a real thing is from a shadow or as waking life is from a dream."...

The new [Narnia] was a deeper country: every rock and flower and blade of grass looked as if it meant more. I can't describe it any better than that: if you ever get there, you will know what I mean.

It was the Unicorn who summed up what everyone was feeling.... "I have come home at last! This is my real country! I belong here. This is the land I have been looking for all my life, though I never knew it till now. The reason why we loved the old Narnia is that it sometimes looked a little like this."[1]

I love the way Pastor Sam Storms puts it:

The fullness of God's presence among his people necessarily demands the banishment of any and all forms of suffering associated with the old creation. Gone forever are the debilitating effects of sin (Rev. 21:3–4). Gone are the tears caused by grief and pain and moral failure (in fulfillment of Isa.

> 25:8). Gone is death, because its source, sin, will have been eradicated. Gone are mourning, crying, and pain. All such experiences are linked to the "first things" which have now "passed away."
>
> The New Jerusalem is said to have "the glory of God" (Rev. 21:11). Whereas in the Old Testament the physical temple was the place where God's glory resided and was manifested, in the new creation God's presence will abide in and with his people. The absence of "night" (Rev. 21:25b) points to the unhindered access to God's radiant presence as well as to the fact that there will be no darkness to dim the brilliance of divine splendor. Indeed, as Revelation 22:5 indicates, the absence of darkness is due to the continual illumination that God himself provides.[2]

When will all this take place? I don't know. Many people have tried to set dates—but the dates they set have come and gone and the old world is still here. As we mentioned previously, Yeshua said that no one knows the day or hour of His return—not even He Himself. He also said He will come "like a thief in the night" (1 Thess. 5:2), which means most people will be caught by surprise. I believe there is a very important reason for this. God doesn't want us to be obsessed by the thought that the end is near. His desire is that we keep working; keep sharing the good news of salvation through His Son; keep feeding the hungry, healing the sick, helping the poor, and generally being "about [our] Father's business" (Luke 2:49, NKJV). He wants us to live as if the Messiah could return at any moment. He wants us to be ready and watching for His return, but not making wrong decisions because we think this world is going to end "a week from Tuesday."

I know there are many questions about the last days that we haven't discussed in this book. These questions and their answers, however, are beyond the scope of this book. My purpose in writing has been to help you understand the vital role the land and people of Israel play in the Messiah's return and the establishment of the messianic age of peace. I also want you to know that no matter what you might be going through right now, a glorious day of joy and restoration is on the way.

Remember when John the Baptist sent some of his disciples to Yeshua to ask if He was, indeed, the Messiah, the Chosen One of God? It seems strange that John would do this. He was, after all, the Messiah's cousin—and he introduced Yeshua to the crowds who were there on the day Yeshua was baptized, saying, "Behold, the Lamb of God who takes away the sin of the world!" (John 1:29).

But John was now facing perilous times. He had been arrested and imprisoned by Herod because he had called the king a sinner for stealing his brother's wife. John knew this was no petty incident that would soon be forgotten. He had insulted the king and queen and was likely to spend the rest of his life in prison.

He had been shaken to the core and needed reassurance that God was still on the throne, and that his cousin was exactly who John had always thought He was, the promised Messiah and Redeemer of Israel. The Bible says that when John's disciples came to Yeshua, they asked Him, "'Are You the Coming One, or do we look for another?' *Yeshua* replied, 'Go report to John what you hear and see: the blind see and the lame walk, those with *tzara'at* [leprosy] are cleansed and the deaf hear, and the dead are raised and the poor have good news proclaimed to them'" (Matt. 11:3–5).

Yeshua was pointing out to John that the kingdom of God had indeed come to the people of Israel. People were being healed and restored, just as they will be when the Messianic age arrives. This was a foretaste of what is about to come in its full glory:

- Those who are blind will have their sight restored.
- Those who are deaf will be able to hear clearly.

- If you have lost a hand, a foot, or another limb, you will be whole when all things are restored.
- If you've lost a child, spouse, or another loved one, they will be restored to you.

Have you suffered the tragedy of losing someone you love to Alzheimer's disease or dementia? What a tragedy when someone you have loved and who has been an important part of your life no longer remembers who you are. But there is hope. Memories and relationships will be restored when the Messiah comes.

Yeshua said, "I make all things new" (Rev. 21:5, NKJV), and I believe He meant exactly what He said. I don't know exactly how He will do it, but I honestly believe He will wipe every tear from our eyes. As Psalm 30:6 says, "Weeping may stay for the night, but joy comes in the morning."

As I've repeatedly stated, these are turbulent times. We live in an age of wars, turmoil, and uncertainty. Things are spiraling out of control, and it is only going to get worse in the days ahead. And yet, if you are walking with God and staying close to Him, you have nothing to fear.

All Will End Well

It's a quiet, calm evening in Phoenix as I write these words. The world seems to be at peace. The desert sky is filling up with stars. There are only a few small puffy clouds overhead, and they are tinged with gold and silver from another gorgeous Arizona sunset. The only sound is a bit of laughter floating in from somewhere down the street.

Everything looks completely normal. But something big is on the way. Something very big. The end of the age is near, and that means Yeshua is coming back soon and will reign from Jerusalem.

This world is about to change in every way possible. If you're ready, this will be extremely good news for you.

Stay alert. Keep watching! And above all, don't give up. Whatever you have gone through, or are going through right now, I assure you, the future will be absolutely magnificent!

NOTES

Introduction

1. Rory Smith and Sewell Chan, "Ariana Grande Manchester Concert Ends in Explosion, Panic and Death," *New York Times*, May 22, 2017, accessed August 6, 2017, https://www.nytimes.com/2017/05/22/world/europe/ariana-grande-manchester-police.html.
2. Alissa J. Rubin, Adam Nossiter, and Christopher Mele, "Scores Die in Nice, France, as Truck Plows Into Bastille Day Crowd," *New York Times*, July 14, 2016, accessed August 6, 2017, https://www.nytimes.com/2016/07/15/world/europe/nice-france-truck-bastille-day.html.
3. "Rocket Attacks on Israel From Gaza," Israeli Defense Forces, accessed August 6, 2017, https://www.idfblog.com/facts-figures/rocket-attacks-toward-israel/.
4. Jan Jaben-Eilon, "Messianic Jewish Groups Claim Rapid Growth," *Jewish Journal*, June 12, 2012, accessed August 6, 2017, http://jewishjournal.com/culture/religion/105069/.
5. Gary Thoma, "The Return of the Jewish Church," *Christianity Today*, September 7, 1998, accessed July 13, 2017, http://www.christianitytoday.com/ct/1998/september7/8ta062.html.
6. Philip Yancey, *The Jesus I Never Knew* (Grand Rapids, MI: Zondervan, 1995), 55.
7. Jessilyn Justice, "Altar of the Lord Rebuilt in Jerusalem—A Sign of the Times?" Charisma News, March 17, 2015, accessed July 10, 2017, http://www.charismanews.com/world/48772-altar-of-the-lord-rebuilt-in-jerusalem-a-sign-of-the-times.

Chapter 1
Key One: The Seed Promise

1. Adolf Hitler, *Mein Kampf*, Jewish Virtual Library, accessed July 11, 2017, http://www.jewishvirtuallibrary.org/excerpts-from-mein-kampf.
2. Ibid.
3. Joseph Goebbels, *The Goebbels Diaries 1942–1943* (New York: L. P. Lochner, Doubleday & Co., 1948), 86, Jewish Virtual Library, accessed July 11, 2017, https://www.jewishvirtuallibrary.org/nazi-statements.

4. Yitzak Arad, Israel Gutman, and Abraham Margaliot, eds., *Documents on the Holocaust* (Jerusalem: University of Nebraska Press, Lincoln and London, and Yad Vashem, 1999), 247–248, Jewish Virtual Library, accessed July 11, 2017, https://www.jewishvirtuallibrary.org/nazi-statements.
5. Elie Wiesel, interview by Georg Klein, Nobelprize.org, December 10, 2004, accessed August 6, 2017, https://www.nobelprize.org/nobel_prizes/peace/laureates/1986/wiesel-interview-transcript.html.
6. Ibid.
7. Henry Ford, *The International Jew: The World's Foremost Problem* vol. 4, *Aspects of Jewish Power in the United States* (Dearborn, MI: The Dearborn Publishing Co., 1922), 46–47.
8. Ibid., 238–39.
9. "Ancient Jewish History: Banking and Bankers," Jewish Virtual Library, accessed August 9, 2017, http://www.jewishvirtuallibrary.org/banking-and-bankers; see also Gregory Myers, "Jewish People Were Forced to Become Money-Lenders," KnowledgeNuts, November 2, 2014, accessed August 6, 2017, http://knowledgenuts.com/2014/11/02/jewish-people-were-forced-to-become-money lenders/.
10. "Anti-Semitism: History of the 'Protocols of the Elders of Zion,'" Jewish Virtual Library, accessed July 11, 2017, http://www.jewishvirtuallibrary.org/the-ldquo-protocols-of-the-elders-of-zion-rdquo.
11. Ibid.
12. Ibid.
13. Martin Luther, *On the Jews and Their Lies* (n.p.: Eulenspiegel Press, 2014), Part IXV, https://tinyurl.com/y8nexaqe.
14. David Horovitz, "ADL Chief Warns Anti-Semitism Worst Since WWII, Even US Jewish Kids Feel Intimidated," *Times of Israel*, July 13, 2015, accessed July 27, 2017, http://www.timesofisrael.com/adl-chief-warns-anti-semitism-worst-since-wwii-even-us-jews-feel-intimidated/.
15. Dakin Andone, "Seattle Synagogue Vandalized with Holocaust Denial Graffiti," CNN, March 10, 2017, accessed August 6, 2017, http://www.cnn.com/2017/03/10/us/seattle-synagogue-vandalized-holocaust-denial/index.html; Shawn Chitnis, "I Cried: Swastikas Spray Painted on Home Investigated as Hate Crime," CBS Denver, June 2, 2017, accessed August 6, 2017, http://denver.cbslocal.com/2017/06/02/aurora-graffiti-swastikas/; Sarah Oehler and Malena Caruso, "Family Staying Positive After Swastika, Vulgar Message Painted on Home," WTOL, updated January 17, 2017, accessed

August 6, 2017, http://www.wtol.com/story/34236823/police-investigating-swastika-vulgar-message-spray-pained-on-.

16. "Why Do People Hate Jews?" Bnei Baruch Kabbalah Education and Research Institute, accessed July 11, 2017, http://www.kabbalah.info/bb/why-do-people-hate-jews/.
17. "Ancient Jewish History: The Great Revolt (99–70 CE)," Jewish Virtual Library, accessed August 6, 2017, http://www.jewishvirtuallibrary.org/the-great-revolt-66-70-ce.
18. "Bar Kochba," New World Encyclopedia, accessed September 5, 2017, http://www.newworldencyclopedia.org/entry/Bar_Kochba.
19. Lewis Loflin and Jerry Darring, "Catholic Timeline of Jew Hatred," accessed July 12, 2017, http://www.sullivan-county.com/news/mine/timeline.htm.
20. Ibid.
21. Ibid.
22. Ibid.
23. Ibid.
24. Ibid.
25. Ibid.
26. Ibid.
27. Ibid.
28. Foundation for the Advancement of Sephardic Studies and Culture, accessed September 5, 2017, http://www.sephardicstudies.org/1492account.html.
29. Loflin and Darring, "Catholic Timeline of Jew Hatred."
30. Ibid.
31. "Why Do People Hate Jews?" Bnei Baruch Kabbalah Education and Research Institute, accessed July 11, 2017, http://www.kabbalah.info/bb/why-do-people-hate-jews/.
32. Ibid.
33. Yancey, *The Jesus I Never Knew*, 55; see also C. H. Dodd, *The Founder of Christianity* (London: The Macmillan Company, 1970), 103.
34. Yancey, *The Jesus I Never Knew*, 55; see also Jaroslav Pelikan, *Jesus Through the Centuries* (New Haven, CT: Yale University Press, 1985), 20.
35. Mark Twain, *The Complete Essays of Mark Twain*, "Concerning the Jews" (New York: Doubleday, 1963), 249.

CHAPTER 2
KEY TWO: THE ABRAHAMIC BLESSING

1. Tim LaHaye and Thomas Ice, *Charting the End Times* (Eugene, OR: Harvest House, 2001), 84.
2. Abraham Lincoln Presidential Library Foundation, accessed July 12, 2017, http://www.alplm.org/272viewessay.aspx?id=800.
3. Dennis Prager, "Those Who Curse the Jews and Those Who Bless Them," DennisPrager.com and Salem National, July 31, 2002, accessed July 12, 2017, http://www.dennisprager.com/those-who-curse-the-jews-and-those-who-bless-them.
4. Ibid.
5. "Action Alert: Fifth-Largest UK Supermarket Chain Launches Anti-Israel Boycott," Stand With Us: Supporting Israel Around the World, accessed August 6, 2017, https://www.standwithus.com/news/article.asp?id=2296.
6. William Koenig, *Eye to Eye: Facing the Consequences of Dividing Israel* (McLean, VA: About Him Publishing, 2006); "Eye to Eye: Facing the Consequences of Dividing Israel–2008," William Koenig, accessed August 6, 2017, https://watch.org/eye-to-eye/eye-eye-facing-consequences-dividing-israel-2008.
7. "1994 Northridge Earthquake," History.com, accessed August 6, 2017, http://www.history.com/topics/1994-northridge-earthquake.
8. Koenig, *Eye to Eye*; "Eye to Eye—Are These Coincidences or God's Wrath?" Issuu.com, accessed August 7, 2017, https://issuu.com/garyboyd2/docs/eye_to_eye.docx; see also "May 3, 1999 Oklahoma/Kansas Tornado Outbreak," National Severe Storms Laboratory, accessed August 6, 2017, http://www.nssl.noaa.gov/about/history/may3rd/.
9. Koenig, *Eye to Eye*; "Eye to Eye: Facing the Consequences of Dividing Israel–2008," William Koenig, accessed August 6, 2017, https://watch.org/eye-to-eye/eye-eye-facing-consequences-dividing-israel-2008.
10. Jonathan Bernis, *A Rabbi Looks at the Last Days* (Grand Rapids, MI: Chosen Books, 2013), 178.
11. "The Miracles of the Six-Day War," Chabad-Lubavitch Media Center, accessed July 12, 2017, http://www.chabad.org/multimedia/timeline_cdo/aid/525341/jewish/Introduction.htm.
12. Ibid.
13. "Israel's War of Independence (1947–1949)," Israel Ministry of Foreign Affairs, accessed July 13, 2017, http://mfa.gov.il/MFA/About

Israel/History/Pages/Israels%20War%20of%20Independence%20-%201947%20-%201949.aspx.

14. "Jewish Biographies: Nobel Prize Laureates," Jewish Virtual Library, accessed July 13, 2017, http://www.jewishvirtuallibrary.org/jewish-nobel-prize-laureates; see also Luana Goriss, "Jewish Nobel Prize Winners," About Religion, accessed August 7, 2017, http://judaism.about.com/od/culture/a/nobel.htm.
15. "Vital Statistics: Jewish Population of the World (1882–Present)," Jewish Virtual Library, accessed August 7, 2017, http://www.jewishvirtuallibrary.org/jewish-population-of-the-world.
16. Derek Prince, *Prophetic Guide to the End Times* (Grand Rapids, MI: Chosen Books, 2008), 157.
17. Ibid.

Chapter 3
Key Three: The New Covenant

1. *The Coptic Encyclopedia, Volume 1*, s.v. "Abd al-Masih al-Isra'ili al-Raqqi," Claremont Colleges Digital Library, accessed August 7, 2017, http://ccdl.libraries.claremont.edu/cdm/ref/collection/cce/id/16; Goodman Lipkind, "Alexander, Michael Solomon," JewishEncyclopedia.com, accessed August 7, 2017, http://www.jewishencyclopedia.com/articles/1148-alexander-michael-solomon; John Tagliabue, "Jean-Marie Lustiger, French Cardinal, Dies at 80," *New York Times*, August 6, 2007, accessed August 7, 2017, http://www.nytimes.com/2007/08/06/world/europe/06lustiger.html; "Chief Rabbi of Rome Becomes Converted to Catholicism; Jewish Community Astonished," JTA, February 15, 1945, accessed August 7, 2017, http://www.jta.org/1945/02/15/archive/chief-rabbi-of-rome-becomes-converted-to-catholicism-jewish-community-astonished.
2. Michael L. Brown, *Answering Jewish Objections to Jesus* (Grand Rapids, MI: Baker Books, 2000), 3.
3. Jonathan Bernis, *A Rabbi Looks at Jesus of Nazareth* (Grand Rapids, MI: Chosen Books, 2011), 58.
4. Brown, *Objections*, 22.
5. Arnold Fruchtenbaum, *Hebrew Christianity: Its Theology, History, and Philosophy* (Washington, DC: Canon Press, 1974), 30–31.
6. *Strong's Exhaustive Concordance of the Bible*, s.v. "*plērōma*," Blue Letter Bible, accessed August 7, 2017, https://www.blueletterbible.org/lang/lexicon/lexicon.cfm?Strongs=G4138&t=KJV.
7. LaHaye and Ice, *Charting*, 84.

8. Sid Roth, *They Thought for Themselves* (Shippensburg, PA: Destiny Image, 2009), chapter 5; see also Sharon Allen, "They Thought for Themselves, Chapter 5," SidRoth.org, February 12, 2005, accessed August 7, 2017, https://sidroth.org/articles/chapter-5-sharon-allen/.
9. Ibid.
10. Ibid.
11. Ibid.
12. Ibid.
13. Ibid.
14. Ibid.
15. Ibid.

Chapter 4
Key Four: The Restoration of Jerusalem

1. Flavius Josephus, *Josephus: The Complete Works*, Christian Classics Ethereal Library, accessed July 28, 2017, https://www.ccel.org/ccel/josephus/complete.iii.vii.iv.html.
2. "History of Jerusalem: Timeline for the History of Jerusalem (4500 BCE–Present)," Jewish Virtual Library, accessed July 14, 2017, http://www.jewishvirtuallibrary.org/timeline-for-the-history-of-jerusalem-4500-bce-present.
3. As quoted in Lily Rothman, "The Story Behind the Democratic Debate's Final Question," *Time*, October 14, 2015, accessed July 14, 2017, http://time.com/4072967/democratic-debate-fdr-quote/.
4. Morris Jastrow Jr., Ira Maurice Price, Marcus Jastrow, Louis Ginzberg, and Duncan B. McDonald, "Tower of Babel," JewishEncyclopedia.com, accessed July 14, 2017, http://www.jewishencyclopedia.com/articles/2279-babel-tower-of.
5. *Strong's Exhaustive Concordance of the Bible*, s.v. "Shem," Blue Letter Bible, accessed July 14, 2017, https://www.blueletterbible.org/lang/Lexicon/Lexicon.cfm?strongs=H8035&t=KJV.
6. Saint Augustine, *City of God*, Book XIV, Chapter 28, Christian Classics Ethereal Library, accessed July 14, 2017, https://www.ccel.org/ccel/schaff/npnf102.iv.XIV.28.html.
7. "History of Jerusalem," Jewish Virtual Library.
8. "Herod's Temple," The Bible Study Site, accessed August 7, 2017, http://www.biblestudy.org/biblepic/picture-of-second-temple-in-jerusalem.html.
9. "Ancient Jewish History: The Two Kingdoms (c.920 BCE–579 BCE)," Jewish Virtual Library, accessed August 7, 2017, http://www.jewishvirtuallibrary.org/the-two-kingdoms-of-israel.

10. "The Jewish Temples: The First Temple—Solomon's Temple," Jewish Virtual Library, accessed August 7, 2017, http://www.jewishvirtual library.org/the-first-temple-solomon-s-temple.
11. "Ancient Jewish History: The Temples (Beit HaMikdash)," Jewish Virtual Library, accessed August 7, 2017, http://www.jewishvirtual library.org/the-jewish-temple-beit-hamikdash.
12. "Ancient Jewish History: The Greeks and the Jews (332–63 BCE)," Jewish Virtual Library, accessed August 7, 2017, http://www.jewish virtuallibrary.org/the-ancient-greeks-and-the-jews-jewish-virtual -library; see also "History of Jerusalem," Jewish Virtual Library.
13. "History of Jerusalem," Jewish Virtual Library; see also "The Maccabees/Hasmoneans: History and Overview (166–129 BCE)," Jewish Virtual Library, accessed August 7, 2017, http://www.jewishvirtual library.org/history-and-overview-of-the-maccabees.
14. "Hellenistic Reform and the Maccabean Revolt," Center for Online Judaic Studies, accessed August 7, 2017, http://cojs.org/hellenistic _reform_and_the_maccabean_revolt/; see also Lawrence H. Schiffman, *From Text to Tradition* (Hoboken, NJ: Ktav Publishing House, 1991).
15. Richard Gottheil and Samuel Krauss, "Pompey the Great," JewishEncyclopedia.com, accessed August 7, 2017, http://www.jewish encyclopedia.com/articles/12264-pompey-the-great; see also Stewart Henry Perowne, "Herod: King of Judaea," Encyclopædia Britannica Online, accessed August 7, 2017, https://www.britannica.com /biography/Herod-king-of-Judaea.
16. Flavius Josephus, *Josephus in Nine Volumes: The Jewish War, Books IV–VII* (London: William Heinemann Ltd., 1961), 7, 1, 1.
17. "Ancient Jewish History: The Bar-Kokhba Revolt (132–135 CE)," Jewish Virtual Library, accessed August 7, 2017, http://www.jewish virtuallibrary.org/the-bar-kokhba-revolt-132-135-ce.
18. "Vital Statistics: Jewish Population of the World (1882–Present)," Jewish Virtual Library, accessed August 7, 2017, http://www.jewish virtuallibrary.org/jewish-population-of-the-world.
19. Benjamin Netanyahu, *A Durable Peace* (New York: Warner Books, 1993), 47; see also Felix Bovet, *Egypt, Palestine and Phoenicia: A Visit to Sacred Lands* (London: 1882).
20. Netanyahu, *A Durable Peace*, 384–85.
21. "Theodor (Binyamin, Ze'ev) Herzl (1860–1904)," Jewish Virtual Library, accessed July 28, 2017, http://www.jewishvirtuallibrary.org /theodor-binyamin-ze-rsquo-ev-herzl.

22. "Theodore Herzl (1860–1904)," Knesset.gov, accessed August 7, 2017, https://www.knesset.gov.il/vip/herzl/eng/Herz_Zion_eng.html.
23. "Theodor Herzl," Jewish Virtual Library.
24. Tibor Krausz, "The Failed Soviet Project to Build a Jewish Homeland in the Russian Far East," *Jerusalem Post*, December 17, 2016, accessed August 7, 2017, http://www.jpost.com/Jerusalem-Report/Books-Hardly-a-land-of-milk-and-honey-472984; see also Ofer Aderet, "The Proposal Balfour Rejected: A Jewish State in the Persian Gulf," Haaretz, April 7, 2014, accessed August 7, 2017, http://www.haaretz.com/jewish/features/.premium-1.584178; Alona Ferber, "This Day in Jewish History//1903: Herzl Proposes Kenya (Not Uganda) as a Safe Haven for the Jews," Haaretz, August 26, 2015, accessed September 6, 2017, http://www.haaretz.com/jewish/this-day-in-jewish-history/1.672878; Saul Jay Singer, "The Plan to Establish a Jewish Homeland in America," JewishPress.com, August 23, 2017, accessed September 6, 2017, http://www.jewishpress.com/indepth/front-page/the-plan-to-establish-a-jewish-homeland-in-america/2017/08/23/; "Proposals for a Jewish State," Wikipedia, accessed September 6, 2017, https://en.wikipedia.org/wiki/Proposals_for_a_Jewish_state.
25. "Balfour Declaration: Text of the Declaration (November 2, 1917)," Jewish Virtual Library, accessed August 7, 2017, http://www.jewishvirtuallibrary.org/text-of-the-balfour-declaration.
26. Ibid.
27. Eli Kavon, "The Balfour Betrayal: How the British Empire Failed Zionism," *Jerusalem Post*, November 2, 2013, accessed August 7, 2017, http://www.jpost.com/Opinion/Op-Ed-Contributors/The-Balfour-betrayal-How-the-British-Empire-failed-Zionism-330440.
28. Netanyahu, *A Durable Peace*, 74–75.
29. Ibid., 75.
30. Ibid., 77.
31. "Jewish Population of Europe in 1945," United States Holocaust Memorial Museum, accessed August 7, 2017, https://www.ushmm.org/wlc/en/article.php?ModuleId=10005687.
32. The International School for Holocaust Studies, "Cyprus Detention Camps," Yad Vashem, accessed August 7, 2017, http://www.yadvashem.org/odot_pdf/Microsoft%20Word%20-%20727.pdf.
33. *Encyclopædia Britannica*, s.v. "United Nations Resolution 181," accessed August 7, 2017, https://www.britannica.com/topic/United-Nations-Resolution-181.

34. "This Day in History: May 14, 1948—State of Israel Proclaimed," History.com, accessed August 7, 2017, http://www.history.com/this-day-in-history/state-of-israel-proclaimed.
35. "The Suez-Sinai Campaign: Egyptian Fedayeen Attacks," Jewish Virtual Library, accessed August 7, 2017, http://www.jewishvirtuallibrary.org/egyptian-fedayeen-attacks-summer-1955.
36. "The Sinai-Suez Campaign: Background and Overview (October–November 1956)," Jewish Virtual Library, accessed August 7, 2017, http://www.jewishvirtuallibrary.org/background-and-overview-sinai-suez-campaign.
37. Ibid.
38. Mitchell D. Bard, *The Complete Idiot's Guide to Middle East Conflict* (Indianapolis, IN: Alpha Books, 1999), 225.
39. Ibid., 226.
40. "The Temple Mount: Mount Moriah," Temple Institute, accessed August 7, 2017, http://templeinstitute.org/temple_mount.htm/The%20Temple%20Mount:%20Mount%20Moriah.
41. Yuval Avivi, "Israeli Institute Prepares Priests for Jerusalem's Third Temple," Temple Institute, April 9, 2014, accessed August 7, 2017, http://www.templeinstitute.org/archive/10-04-14.htm.
42. Ibid.

Chapter 5
Key Five: The Gospel to the Jew First

1. *Strong's Exhaustive Concordance of the Bible*, s.v. "ethnos," Blue Letter Bible, accessed August 7, 2017, https://www.blueletterbible.org/lang/Lexicon/Lexicon.cfm?strongs=G1484&t=KJV.
2. Derek Leman, *The World to Come* (Clarksville, MD: Lederer Books, 2008), 34.
3. Ibid.
4. Ibid., 29, 35.

Chapter 6
Key Six: Bringing Life From the Dead

1. Katie Rogers, "Bride Is Walked Down Aisle by the Man Who Got Her Father's Donated Heart," *New York Times*, August 8, 2016, accessed August 7, 2017, https://www.nytimes.com/2016/08/09/fashion/weddings/bride-is-walked-down-aisle-by-the-man-who-got-her-fathers-donated-heart.html.
2. Amy Wadas, "Man Who Received Bride's Father's Heart to Walk Her Down Aisle," CBS Pittsburgh, August 5, 2016, accessed August

7, 2017, http://pittsburgh.cbslocal.com/2016/08/05/man-who-received-brides-fathers-heart-to-walk-her-down-aisle/.

3. Lindsey Bever, "'I Could Feel His Heartbeat': Bride Asks Her Dad's Heart Recipient to Walk Her Down the Aisle," *Washington Post*, August 9, 2016, accessed August 7, 2017, https://www.washingtonpost.com/news/inspired-life/wp/2016/08/08/i-could-feel-his-heartbeat-bride-asks-her-dads-heart-recipient-to-walk-her-down-the-aisle/?utm_term=.706373df8a2e.
4. Wadas, "Man."
5. Rogers, "Bride."
6. Prince, *Prophetic Guide*, 151.
7. Rom Kampeas, "Has the Time Come to Accept Messianic Jews?," *Times of Israel*, November 20, 2013, accessed July 18, 2017, http://www.timesofisrael.com/has-the-time-come-to-accept-messianic-jews/.
8. David Lazarus, "Messianic Organization Awarded in Israeli Knesset," *Israel Today*, July 13, 2016, accessed July 18, 2017, http://www.israeltoday.co.il/NewsItem/tabid/178/nid/29610/Default.aspx.
9. Chris Mitchell, "Visions of Jesus Stir Muslim Hearts," CBN News, accessed July 18, 2017, http://www1.cbn.com/onlinediscipleship/visions-of-jesus-stir-muslim-hearts.
10. Ibid.
11. Ibid.
12. Ibid.
13. Alex Crain, "Millions of Muslims Converting to Christianity," Crosswalk.com, July 29, 2014, accessed July 18, 2017, http://www.christianity.com/blogs/alex-crain/millions-of-muslims-converting-to-christ.html.

CHAPTER 7
KEY SEVEN: THE RESTORATION OF ALL THINGS

1. Maimonides, Commentary on Mishnah, Sanhedrin 10:1.
2. Babylonian Talmud: Tractate Sanhedrin 98a, viewed online at http://www.come-and-hear.com/sanhedrin/sanhedrin_98.html.
3. C. S. Lewis, *Mere Christianity* (New York: Harper One, 1952), XX.
4. *Wikipedia: The Free Encyclopedia*, s.v. "Jesus Movement," accessed August 7, 2017, https://en.wikipedia.org/wiki/Jesus_movement; see also Stella Lau, *Popular Music in Evangelical Youth Culture* (New York: Routledge, 2013), 33; Bruce David Forbes and Jeffrey H. Mahan, *Religion and Popular Culture in America* (Oakland, CA: University of California Press, 2005), 103; Eileen Luhr, *Witnessing*

Suburbia: Conservatives and Christian Youth Culture (Oakland, CA: University of California Press, 2009).

5. Benjamin Glatt, "Today in History: Founding of Tel Aviv," *Jerusalem Post*, April 11, 2016, accessed August 7, 2017, http://www.jpost.com/Christian-News/Today-in-history-Founding-of-Tel-Aviv-450852.
6. Amanda Borschel-Dan, "Twenty-Five Years Later, Russian Speakers Still the 'Other' in Israel, Says MK," , September 1, 2016, accessed August 7, 2017, http://www.timesofisrael.com/25-years-later-russian-speakers-still-the-other-in-israel-says-mk/.
7. Conor Gaffey and Jack Moore, "Why Ethiopian Jews Face Discrimination and Police Brutality in Israel," *Newsweek*, September 26, 2016, accessed August 7, 2017, http://www.newsweek.com/2016/10/07/why-ethiopian-jews-israel-face-discrimination-racism-police-brutality-502697.html.
8. Doug Criss and Carma Hassan, "Anti-Semitic Incidents Rose a Whopping 86 Percent in the First Three Months of 2017," CNN, April 24, 2017, accessed July 28, 2017, http://www.cnn.com/2017/04/24/us/antisemitic-incidents-reports-trnd/index.html.
9. Abraham X. Foxman, "Rising Anti-Semitism in Europe: History Repeating Once Again," *Huffington Post*, accessed July 28, 2017, http://www.huffingtonpost.com/abraham-h-foxman/rising-anti-semitism-in-e_b_7835610.html.
10. "Fact Sheet—Latest Statistics on the Status of the AIDS Epidemic," UNAIDS, accessed August 7, 2017, http://www.unaids.org/en/resources/fact-sheet.
11. Steve Almasy and Carma Hassan, "South Carolina School Shooting: Six-Year-Old Victim Dies," CNN, October 2, 2016, accessed August 7, 2017, http://www.cnn.com/2016/10/01/us/south-carolina-elementary-school-shooting-victim/index.html.
12. "Hurricane Matthew Recap: Destruction From the Caribbean to the United States," Weather.com, October 9, 2016, accessed July 19, 2017, https://weather.com/storms/hurricane/news/hurricane-matthew-bahamas-florida-georgia-carolinas-forecast; see also Pam Wright, "Haitians Struggle to Survive in Wake of Hurricane Matthew: 'They Are Hungry and Thirsty and Some Are Getting Angry,'" Weather.com, October 13, 2016, accessed August 7, 2017, https://weather.com/news/news/hurricane-matthew-haiti-latest-news-0; David Lawler, Chris Graham, and James Rothwell, "Hurricane Matthew: Two Million People in US Urged to Evacuate as Barack Obama Warns of 'Serious Storm,'" *Telegraph*, October 6, 2016, accessed August 7, 2017, http://www.telegraph.co.uk/news/2016/10/05

/hurricane-matthew-eleven-dead-as-un-warns-of-worst
-humanitarian/.

13. Kevin Sullivan and Mark Berman, "Texas Officials Say At Least Nine Dead as Harvey Flooding Continues," *Washington Post*, August 28, 2017, accessed September 6, 2017, https://www.washingtonpost.com/news/post-nation/wp/2017/08/28/harvey-may-force-30000-people-into-shelters-while-flooding-will-linger-officials-warn/?utm_term=.020b4abb48e6; see also Lla Eustachewich, "Harvey Wiped Out As Many As 40,000 Homes in Houston," *New York Post*, August 30, 2017, accessed September 6, 2017, http://nypost.com/2017/08/30/up-to-40000-homes-wiped-out-by-harvey/; Paul O'Donnell, "Tracking Harvey's Toll: 'This Is the Costliest and Worst Natural Disaster in American History," *Dallas News*, September 1, 2017, accessed September 6, 2017, https://www.dallasnews.com/news/harvey/2017/08/31/tracking-harveys-toll-costliest-worst-natural-disaster-american-history; Todd C. Frankel, Avi Selk, and David A. Fahrenthold, "Residents Warned to 'Get Out or Die' as Harvey Unleashes New Waves of Punishing Rains and Flooding," *Washington Post*, August 30, 2017, accessed September 6, 2017, https://www.washingtonpost.com/news/post-nation/wp/2017/08/30/harvey-again-makes-landfall-this-time-as-a-tropical-storm-near-cameron-la/?utm_term=.19cd092a7687.
14. "Dust Covered Painting in Attic Found to Be a Masterpiece," *Telegraph*, November 23, 2008, accessed July 19, 2017, http://www.telegraph.co.uk/news/uknews/3507130/Dust-covered-painting-in-attic-found-to-be-a-masterpiece.html.
15. Ibid.
16. Alfred Tennyson, "Morte D'Arthur," from *Poems*, 4th edition (London: Moxon, 1845), accessed July 19, 2017, https://library.sc.edu/spcoll/britlit/tenn/morte.html.

Conclusion
Fight the Good Fight

1. C. S. Lewis, *The Last Battle* (New York: Collier, 1956), 168–71.
2. Sam Storms, *The Restoration of All Things*, The Gospel Coalition Booklets (Wheaton, IL: Crossway Books, 2011), 25.